LOONY LAWSUITS

Loony Lawsuits

MATT SILVERMAN

BARNES
&NOBLE
BOOKS
NEW YORK

I raise a scalding-hot cup of coffee
in thanks to Justin Mitchell, Bill Locke, Bob Dippo,
Heather Russell-Revesz, Rick Campbell, and,
as always, Deborah Silverman.

This edition published by Barnes & Noble by arrangement
with the author

2003 Barnes & Noble Books

Text design by Leah Lococo

ISBN: 0-7607-3893-9

Printed and bound in the United States of America

03 04 05 06 07 MP 9 8 7 6 5 4 3 2 1

TABLE OF CONTENTS

OPENING STATEMENT 7

HE SAID, SHE SAID 12

JAILHOUSE JURISPRUDENCE 24

JOHN Q. PUBLIC GETS HIS DAY IN COURT 40

SCHOOL DAYS, SCHOOL DAYS,
GOOD OLD GOLDEN RULE DAYS 54

IT'S NOT ABOUT THE MONEY 64

WHAT'S UP, DOC? 76

TRAFFIC JAM IN THE COURTROOMS 86

FAME AND FORTUNE 98

A FOOL FOR A CLIENT 114

BUT IT WASN'T MY FAULT 124

TOO LOONY 136

SOURCES AND ADDITIONAL READING 141

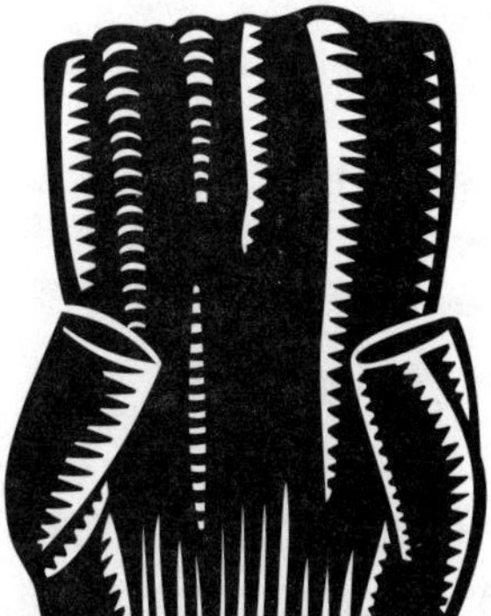

OPENING STATEMENT

Q. How many lawyers does it take to screw in a light bulb?

A. Three. The first climbs a ladder and holds the bulb in the socket, the second turns the ladder in circles, and the third sues the ladder manufacturer for $10 million when the first lawyer falls down.

LUDICROUS LAWSUITS have been filed and outrageous judgments have been handed down in record numbers in the past few years. Calls to end these abuses have been heard in Washington and in statehouses around the country. The political parties have drawn up sides, each condemning the naked greed of the other side. Republicans (and business interests) have generally favored "tort reform," and the Democrats (and trial lawyers) have usually championed "victims' rights."

Almost one hundred of these loony lawsuits are described in this book. Some involve absurd disputes between parties who should never have been in court. Others include outlandish settlements, preposterous behavior, or just plain silliness by the lawyers, plaintiffs, defendants, and witnesses—even by the judges. But each includes an element or two that is so absurd, you just have to laugh. (So that everyone is laughing, the names of many of the plaintiffs and defendants have been changed.)

The most famous (or infamous) loony lawsuit is the case involving Stella Liebeck, a little old lady who was awarded millions of dollars from McDonald's after what seemed to be a minor incident. Turns out there is more to her story.

Liebeck, seventy-nine, spilled coffee from a McDonald's drive-through on herself in 1992. Sitting in the passenger seat of a stationary car, she held the Styrofoam cup between her knees and opened the lid to add cream and sugar. The contents spilled into her lap, causing third-degree burns over 6 percent of her body. Liebeck endured a week in the hospital, several skin grafts, and permanent scarring. According to the Washington State Trial Lawyer's Association, she sued only after McDonald's offered to pay just $800 of her $11,000 medical bill. The company also rejected a $250,000 settlement, which was recommended by a mediator. So Stella sued.

A key issue in the trial was evidence that 700 people had been burned by McDonald's coffee in the past decade, many seriously. Her lawyers claimed that the company served coffee much hotter than other restaurants, had ignored hundreds of injuries caused by this practice, and refused to reduce the temperature of their coffee to prevent severe burns. A jury found Liebeck partly at fault and awarded her $160,000 in compensatory damages. But the jurors also slapped McDonald's with a $2.7 million award for punitive damages. A judge reduced that amount to $480,000, and then the parties eventually settled out of court for an undisclosed sum.

Loony lawsuit? Outrageous judgment? You decide. But most people will agree that there is something wrong with a system in which a new lawsuit is filed every couple of seconds. Many of these suits are ludicrous, and the cost of the litigation is enormous. According to a study by the actuarial advisor Tillinghast-Towers Perrin, lawsuits cost Americans more than $150 billion a year, over 2.5 times the amount we spend annually on police and fire protection. Joseph Perkins of the *San Diego Union-Tribune* even created the "Stella Awards" to highlight the most outlandish lawsuits of the year. The Michigan Lawsuit Abuse Watch has bestowed similar honors, termed the "Whiplash! Awards."

Filings by prison inmates provide one of the richest veins of loony lawsuits. In fact, many states spend a huge portion of their justice budget on prisoner lawsuits, some substantive, many frivolous. A few years ago the attorneys general of New York and Minnesota announced their top lists of frivolous lawsuits. In these and other states, inmates have demanded damages and filed suits alleging the following:

1. The prison barber gave bad haircuts.
2. The towels were the wrong color.
3. The ice cream snacks were mostly melted.
4. The menus included an insufficient variety of beans, too much bologna, or not enough salsa.
5. The scrambled eggs were overcooked.
6. Meat and vegetables were served on the same plate.

7. Creamy peanut butter was offered instead of crunchy.
8. A toilet seat was too cold.
9. Inmates who work as paralegals in the prison law library should earn as much as lawyers earn.
10. Prisons should provide salad bars ($129 million in damages requested).
11. Limits on Kool-Aid refills constitute "cruel and unusual punishment."
12. Pairs of issued underwear were too tight (also "cruel and unusual")

And that's just a dirty dozen. Hundreds more are in the record, a few of which are in the section of this book titled "Jailhouse Jurisprudence."

Romances gone sour, unsatisfied customers, celebrity stalkers, and traffic accidents are all responsible for many loony lawsuits. So are "frequent filers," disgruntled employees, unhappy patients, peeved pet owners, foolish lawyers, and old-fashioned gold diggers. Suits from all of these sources (and more) are included here.

Finally, the worldwide rumor mill, also known as the Internet, is full of stories about loony lawsuits that sound real, but never existed. Strictly fiction. Totally bogus. Check out the section "Too Loony" on these made-up lawsuits at the end of this book. As loony as the phony lawsuits are, you may find the real ones to be even loonier.

PART ONE

He Said, She Said

Lawsuit:

A machine you go into as a pig and come out of as a sausage.

—Ambrose Bierce,

"The Devil's Dictionary"

ISN'T THAT SPECIAL?

In 1990 Melanie Carswell of Puyallup, Washington, sued the driver of a car in which she had been riding. Melanie had been injured by shattered glass when a third party threw a rock, breaking a window in the car. The driver Melanie sought damages from was her husband, Peter, based on his negligent failure to protect her safety while they were on vacation in Miami.

Peter had a bad case of a disease that often affects males: he hated to stop for directions, and when he did stop, he didn't listen. He also had a syndrome that is specific to husbands: he got lost, ignored his wife's suggestions, and refused to let her see the map. The happy couple found themselves lost, late, and angry in "a very ugly part of town." They parked briefly and an assailant broke their car window, robbed them, and Melanie wound up with a severe arm injury. So she sued her old man.

In 1992 Judge Sauriol of the Pierce County Superior Court entered a summary judgment in Peter's favor, but Melanie wasn't finished. She appealed. Melanie said that a "special relationship" existed between her and Peter, not as husband and wife but as driver and passenger, which gave rise to a legal duty on Peter's part to afford Melanie "a right to protection."

Over two years later, the Washington Court of Appeals affirmed the lower court's judgment. It held that no "special relationship" existed that would give rise to a duty on the part of the husband as driver to protect his wife as passenger.

WOULDN'T YOU REALLY RATHER DRIVE A BUICK?

Wanda and Jim Olsen were the joint owners of a 1977 Pontiac that the couple had purchased for $600. They both used it, though not always for the same purpose.

One night in 1988, Jim drove the Pontiac to pick up a prostitute. He parked on a dark Detroit street and began to receive the professional service he required. However, the unsuspecting john was being observed by a police officer, who arrested Olsen for gross indecency, a misdemeanor to which he later pleaded guilty. He was fined $250, required to perform community service, and the car was forfeited to the state. Under Michigan statute, a vehicle used for prostitution can be declared a nuisance and taken, even if the owner is unaware of the criminal activity.

Wanda, though not objecting to the Pontiac's forfeiture, wanted her 50 percent share of the proceeds of its sale (after administrative and court costs were deducted). She sued the state. Wanda said that Jim had her general consent to use the car, but she sure as heck didn't know about or approve of the illegal use. She wanted half the money. The trial court said no, and the Michigan Supreme Court affirmed.

The case went all the way to the United States Supreme Court, which found in 1996 that since Wanda had permitted Jim to use her property, she was subject to its forfeiture when he used the car for illegal purposes.

MANDY'S REVENGE

Judge Jeffrey Ammons of the Arizona Court of Appeals sued singer Barry Manilow in 1994. The judge claimed that attending a Manilow concert in Tucson the previous year damaged his hearing permanently and resulted in a constant, painful ringing in his ears.

Ammons said, "in our society, large industries like the music business do not listen to you unless you file a lawsuit." In 1997 the singer agreed to donate $5,000 to an ear-disorder group, the American Tinnitus Association, to settle the claim.

The judge's wife was relieved. "She loves Barry," Ammons explained.

GET ME TO THE CHURCH ON TIME

Two kids in love, Tim Thompson and Pauline Fairlie, became husband and wife, but their trip down the aisle wasn't a smooth one. According to Associated Press reports, Thompson, forty-eight, sued Fairlie, forty-nine, in November 1991 in Monticello, Kentucky, for backing out of their planned wedding. Thompson, a truck driver, sued for breach of promise, demanding that she had better marry him or return the $400 engagement ring. Fairlie denied having promised to marry Thompson and alleged that he had harassed her.

Well, that must have been the basis for a beautiful relationship, because he dropped the suit the next February. It seems the lovebirds had rescheduled their nuptials.

Guess what? She apparently got cold feet again in July, and the twice bit, but not shy groom went for the tactic that worked so well the first time. He asked the court (unsuccessfully) to reinstate his suit.

On September 1, 1992 they finally tied the knot. After the wedding, Mr. Thompson said, "We just aim to deal with our little problems and get on with our life . . . Let bygones be bygones." Mrs. Thompson said she still was a little peeved about her spouse's romantic strategies.

NO KNOCK

According to 1992 Pennsylvania police reports, Charles Fox drank about twenty double rum and colas at a local American Legion post's bar. He proceeded to drive to the factory where his estranged wife Karli and her boyfriend were working. Armed and dangerous, Fox blasted his way through a locked door and fired at the hapless boyfriend. He then rammed his car into a police cruiser while making his getaway, leaving an officer wounded. Fox was soon arrested and charged with attempted homicide.

A little marital spat like this might just bring a couple back together, it seems—maybe because they have something else in common. Maybe that something else is gall. The Foxes filed suits against both the American Legion club and her now former-employer, Binney and Smith, Inc., the one hundred-year-old company that makes Crayola crayons. Charles said the legion hall served him so much booze that it sent him on the violent rampage. He said a female bartender took advantage of his fragile "emotional state of being" by insisting that he drink more. I'm a victim, Fox said.

Karli claimed that the company should have stopped her boyfriend, a co-worker, from becoming her friend, then seducing her. If Binney and Smith had acted properly, she said, they would never have begun their affair. Karli held the crayon manufacturer liable for the shooting. She claimed that her boyfriend planned to "play on her weaknesses and extract information from her concerning her personal life . . . which would ultimately lead into having sex." According to her suit, Binney and Smith was guilty of not realizing that her illicit relationship would drive Charles Fox insane. (Karli's lawsuit was soon dropped and the Foxes reconciled.)

OEDIPUS WRECKS

In 1992 a Cleveland auto mechanic named Bradley Maples sued an elderly customer he had known for years, asking damages of $2,613. He alleged that she had failed to pay him for repairs he made to her pickup truck. Shortly thereafter, the woman filed a counterclaim, offering as evidence the many services she had provided him free over the years, some of which included acting as his nurse, cook, and even his bail bondsman.

The woman that Maples sued was his mother, Ethel, age seventy-eight, who said she didn't want to cause legal problems for the boy, but what could she do? Ohio's mothers rallied to her support. A mother of three said, "Two thousand dollars doesn't even begin to touch what a mother shells out on a child." Another agreed, "Her son can't fix his mother's car? What's she going to do, buy a new one? Your son's an auto mechanic, the least he can do is fix your car for free."

In her counter suit Ethel also asked the court to administer to Bradley "the whipping that he so rightly needs and which I failed to give him as a child." The judge dismissed the son's claim, but declined to provide Bradley with the spanking his mother suggested.

FOOT FOUL

Reuters reported in late 2001 that Ben Garcia was suing a stripper and her strip club in Vancouver, British Columbia, for unspecified damages. The suburban patron claimed he was kicked in the face by the "reckless" exotic dancer, identified only as "Jane Doe."

And you thought these things only happened in the litigious United States.

Garcia said the Top Hat Motor Inn negligently failed to post prominent signs warning front-row customers of the risks of sitting up close and personal. According to the suit, Garcia's nose was fractured when the dancer kicked him with her high heel as she swung around a pole. (Must not have been a hockey player to grumble about injuries from a woman's dainty foot.) He also complained of blurred vision, headaches, and breathing difficulties.

Among the many mysteries in this drama is, how did he explain his injuries to his wife?

SHORT FUSE

Susan Romish lit a decorative candle to enhance the mood at Trumpets Restaurant in Ottawa County, Michigan, in 1998. Trouble was, it wasn't her candle. The other trouble was, it wasn't a candle at all. It was a large firecracker that exploded in her hand and caused severe injuries. So she reacted like anyone chastened by such a blunder would; she sued the people from whom she had taken the "candle" originally.

The *Holland Sentinel* explained that Steve and Lauren Fisher had hired Romish, forty-four, to clean their Grand Haven condominium. In her suit Romish accused the Fishers of negligence for leaving the firecracker in a cupboard. Romish informed the court that she was instructed to clean up the condo and remove any "miscellaneous items left behind." She found what she assumed was a decorative candle in a kitchen cabinet and "kept it and took it with her." Later, at the restaurant, Romish lit the firecracker she had mistaken for a candle, causing serious injuries.

That's not the way it happened, said the Fishers. First of all, they responded, the candle wasn't hers; she shouldn't have taken it. They had placed the "huge firecracker" in a cupboard to keep it away from children, after partygoers had left it at their home. It was Romish's own poor judgment, not any negligence on their part that caused the injuries she suffered.

The judge agreed with the condo owners. Romish had asked for more than $25,000, but the circuit court dismissed her suit.

PART TWO

Jailhouse Jurisprudence

I know how men in exile feed
on dreams of hope.

–Aeschylus

CLOSER MY GOD TO THEE

Illinois inmate Frank Wilson was serving thirty years for attempted murder and other violent crimes when he submitted a lawsuit in the United States District Court for the Northern District of Illinois in Rockford. He sued the state's Department of Corrections and thirteen other defendants for about $14 million. Wilson charged the defendants with violating his First Amendment right to religious freedom by preventing him from worshipping in his birthday suit. "I'm not really sure why I have to be naked," he told the *Rockford Register-Star.* "It brings me closer to God."

Wilson said his Technicians of the Sacred religion, which is described as "neo-African," requires nude worship and voodoo chanting. Wilson, who is white and tattooed with a Confederate flag, also complained that the Dixon Correctional Center would not let him order voodoo books.

Corrections Department spokesman Nic Howell said, "Nothing surprises me. It is not uncommon for people to sue us for just about anything." Wilson's suit reminded him of one inmate who sued because a bird flew in his cell window, stealing his peanut butter and jelly sandwich, and another (male) maximum-security prisoner who demanded the right to wear makeup and a training bra.

SPLITTING THE SHEETS

In February 1996 David Earl Dempsey was in an Arizona prison, suspected of having mugged a seventy-six-year-old woman. (He was later convicted.) In an unsuccessful suicide attempt, Dempsey leapt from a window in the Pima County Jail while trying to hang himself. The inmate sustained numerous injuries when he hit a concrete floor after the bed sheet to which he tied himself failed to hold him.

The Arizona Daily Star and the *Tucson Weekly* reported that the thirty-seven-year-old inmate then filed suit against Arizona, Pima County, and Tucson officials for damages related to the injuries he suffered.

Dempsey succeeded on a second suicide attempt, and the lawsuit was dismissed.

STOP ME BEFORE I SUE AGAIN

In February 1997 the United States Court of Appeals for the Fourth Circuit limited the ability of a Chesapeake, Virginia inmate, John Bell Miller, to file any more lawsuits. Miller, aka Old Spirit Potter, lodged twenty-nine appeals before that court in 1995-96 alone, possibly making him the most frequent litigant in the circuit. Essentially all of his complaints were about some aspect of prison conditions. None were ever found by any court to have any merit.

His looniest lawsuit came in 1996 when he filed a $5 million lawsuit against himself, accusing John Bell Miller of violating his own civil rights and religious beliefs. He also sued himself for getting so drunk that he committed the crimes that landed him in jail. Miller wrote, "I want to pay myself $5 million but ask the state to pay it in my behalf since I can't work and am a ward of the state."

The court of appeals noted that "in an apparent effort to undermine the legal system that incarcerated him . . . [he] has complained about all aspects of his legal treatment and prison conditions including food, clothing, access to and the poor condition of the prison's law library, mail delivery, hot water, improper placement of a mirror for the handicapped, phones, canteen needs, art supplies, mental stress, and the price of coffee." Miller demanded "$1 million for mental cruelty and cruel and unusual punishment" because the prison nurses said "no" when he requested that his meals contain "extra meat" or "vitamins in place of vegetables." When this case was dismissed as frivolous, Miller responded by suing the victim of the crime for which he had been jailed.

SOMETIMES EVEN THE NAME OF THE SUIT IS LOONY

Edmond Frank MacGillivray Jr. filed a complaint alleging that he had endured over sixty civil rights violations in a series of incidents arising from a nonviolent protest in 1986. He sought damages of almost, but not quite $2 billion, specifically $1,998,000,000. The plaintiff alleged that he had begun demonstrating peacefully on the steps of Michigan's capitol, and then was taken into custody on trespassing charges when he would not produce his name or identification to the police's satisfaction.

MacGillivray said he had been possessed by the devil. Concerned about MacGillivray's mental state, a district court judge placed him in an observation cell where the inmate began chanting and pounding his head on walls. He attempted to commit suicide by slitting his wrists and was treated for his wounds and psychological condition.

MacGillivray recovered and sued from his jail cell. The heading of the legal document that named the parties was as follows:

> I AM THE BEAST SIX SIX SIX OF THE LORD OF HOSTS IN EDMOND FRANK MACGILLIVRAY JR NOW. I AM THE BEAST SIX SIX SIX OF THE LORD OF HOSTS IEFMJN. I AM THE BEAST SIX SIX SIX OF THE LORD OF HOSTS. I AM THE BEAST SIX SIX SIX OTLOHIEFMJN. I AM THE BEAST SSSOTLOHIEFMJN. I AM THE BEAST SIX SIX SIX. BEAST SIX SIX SIX LORD, Plaintiff,
>
> v.
>
> MICHIGAN STATE POLICE; CITY POLICE OF LANSING; STATE OF MICHIGAN; INGHAM COUNTY 54A DISTRICT COURT; AND INGHAM COUNTY JAIL, Defendants.

Ultimately, the court granted a motion by the defendants to dismiss.

WHEN FLOSS IS OUTLAWED . . .

In 1994 Phillip Jones was in the South Central Regional Jail in Charleston, West Virginia, serving time for manslaughter and armed robbery. The inmate busied himself by braiding dental floss into a rope, which he used to scale an eighteen-foot wall and escape from a recreation yard. (Jones apparently also used a small piece of a hacksaw blade to saw through the chain-link fence above the wall.)

Sales of dental floss at the prison were quickly suspended there, but Maine officials were one step ahead. They had already prohibited inmates from having dental floss, to prevent just such a daring escape. However, Portland inmate William Friar sued the Pine Tree State, claiming that its rule of zero tolerance for dental floss inhibited his right to fight tooth decay.

NOW HE COULD PROBABLY GET HBO

While in custody in New Jersey in 1962, Ted Spector was taken to the Eye, Ear and Speech Clinic of Newark. Thirteen years later he sued the state for $12 million. Spector said the clinic had unlawfully injected him in the left eye with a radium electric beam. Consequently, he claimed, someone was talking to him from the inside of his brain.

The United States District Court had a few words of technical advice for the plaintiff. Judge Biunno said that, "Just as Mr. Houdini has so far failed to establish communication from the spirit world (see E. L. Doctorow, *'Ragtime'*, [New York: Random House, 1974], pp. 166-169), so the decades of scientific experiments and statistical analysis have failed to establish the existence of 'extrasensory perception' (ESP). But, taking the facts as pleaded, and assuming them to be true, they show a case of presumably unlicensed radio communication, a matter which comes within the sole jurisdiction of the Federal Communications Commission . . . And even aside from that, [Spector] could have blocked the broadcast to the antenna in his brain simply by grounding it. (See, for example, Ghirardi, *'Modern Radio Servicing'*, [New York: Radio and Technical Publishing Co., 1935], 572 ff.). Just as delivery trucks for oil and gasoline are 'grounded' against the accumulation of charges of static electricity, so on the same principle

[Spector] might have pinned to the back of a trouser leg a short chain of paper clips so that the end would touch the ground and prevent anyone from talking to him inside his brain."

The complaint was dismissed for statute of limitation and jurisdictional reasons.

MUST HAVE BEEN A VERY GOOD T-SHIRT BUSINESS

In 1994 Hector Gonzalez was convicted of murdering New York City undercover detective Luis Lopez during a raid. He was sentenced to a term of fifty-five years to life. The next year Gonzalez sued the New York Police Department for $3 million, claiming that other officers hurt him during the arrest.

Some of the $3 million was for lost earnings, despite evidence that Gonzalez's occupation was selling illegal drugs. He claimed to be an employee of a T-shirt store.

(In early 2002 New York State Supreme Court Justice Marcy L. Kahn overturned Gonzalez's conviction. Despite statements from the lead prosecutor and others, she accepted the testimony of Gonzalez's mother and a codefendant's lawyer, that the judge who heard the murder case fell asleep briefly during jury selection. The city has appealed.)

PRODUCE THE BODY

Lots of inmates—maybe most of them—claim they were sent to jail wrongly. But James Upton put a new spin on the old mistaken identity game. Upton was imprisoned at the United States Penitentiary in Marion, Illinois, after a conviction in Wisconsin. Upon his conviction in a jury trial, Judge Robert Landry had sentenced him to two life sentences plus 175 years for murder, armed robbery, and attempted murder.

Upton filed a habeas corpus action attacking the validity of that conviction. Among other claims he stated the following:

1. He was not James Upton but the "Prophet Muhammad," convicted under the wrong name.
2. He was not the same person who was convicted by the jury, but Judge Landry mistakenly sent him to jail.
3. His case was "fixed" because he is a Muslim and all of the jurors who convicted him were Christians.
4. Islamic law, not the laws of the "Masonic Regime" that held him hostage, should have governed his trial.
5. As a member of the Nation of Islam, he should have received the benefit of Saudi Arabia's foreign state immunity.

The United States District Court for the Southern District of Illinois found that central to Upton's claims was "his statement that he is the prophet Muhammad, the authority of Islam in the East and West and presumably the same prophet Muhammad who died in the year 632. It might appear that this action is frivolous and subject to . . . dismissal for that reason alone . . . but it is not the place of a federal court to decide which is the true faith or who is a true prophet . . . We will, therefore, accept [the] plaintiff's claims in good faith in making our threshold determination."

Despite accepting the prisoner's claims to be Muhammad, the court dismissed the claim on procedural grounds. It passed the buck back to the state courts, ruling that Upton had to exhaust all available remedies there before applying for habeas corpus in the federal courts.

ON, COMET! ON, CUPID!

Donnie Clubb was serving fourteen years for robbery and assault in an Amarillo prison, but he felt he'd been cheated. Not by the Texas justice system, but by *Penthouse*. He sued the nudie magazine for $500,000 in damages, alleging that one of its December pictorial layouts was insufficiently revealing. The disappointing images of Paula Jones, whose fifteen minutes in the spotlight came when she filed a sexual harassment suit against President Clinton, caused the inmate to be "very mentally hurt and angered."

Clubb, who identified himself in the suit as the "Minister of Law of the Mandingo Warriors" prison gang, lost again. In 2000 U.S. District Judge Sam Sparks dismissed the suit and fined Clubb $250 for filing a frivolous legal motion. His judgment took the form of a brief poem that read in part:

"'Twas the night before Christmas and all through
the prison
Inmates were planning their new porno mission.
. . . The minute his *Penthouse* issue arrived,
The Minister ripped it open to see what was inside.
But what to his wondering eyes should appear—
Not Paula Jones' promised privates, but only her rear.
Life has its disappointments. Some come out of the blue
But that doesn't mean a prisoner should sue."

PART THREE

John Q. Public Gets His Day in Court

I do not find fault with equality for drawing men into the pursuit of forbidden pleasures, but for absorbing them entirely in the search for the pleasures that are permitted.

–Alexis de Toqueville,

"Democracy in America"

ATTACK ON BIG MAC

In July 2002, 270-pound Marcus Hairston filed a class action lawsuit in the New York State Supreme Court in the Bronx. On behalf of other obese New Yorkers who eat fat-drenched burgers, fries, and fried chicken, Hairston claimed that Burger King, Wendy's, McDonald's, and KFC jeopardized his health. "They never explained to me what I was eating," he complained.

Even after his heart attack, admits the fifty-six-year-old Hairston, he ate the greasy fast-food up to five times a week. But the companies failed to adequately disclose either their food's ingredients or the risks of overeating, he says. A diabetic, Hairston claims the restaurant chains were negligent and "profited enormously" from selling him finger-lickin' foods that are loaded with fat, salt, sugar, and cholesterol.

John Doyle, a restaurant industry spokesman, said that to win the suit Hairston would "ha[ve] to convince a jury or a judge that people are too stupid to feed themselves or their children. If people are so stupid, should they be allowed to vote or go to work in the morning?"

A related class-action lawsuit, which blamed McDonald's for health problems in New York kids, was dismissed early in 2003. One 278-pound thirteen-year-old plaintiff had said he ate at McDonald's three or four times a week. His attorney (who also represented Hairston) said the high fat, high cholesterol food at McDonald's was "insipid" and "toxic."

Maybe so, but the supersized young plaintiffs should have known better. "Nobody is forced to eat at McDonald's," said U.S. District Court Judge Robert Sweet. "It is not the place of the law to protect (consumers) from their own excesses."

PLAINTIFFS IN A PICKLE

Janella Swanson claimed she suffered a second-degree burn and was permanently scarred by a defective and dangerous product. She said an extremely hot piece of pickle fell on her chin at a McDonald's in Knoxville, Tennessee.

In October 1999, after the perilous pickle tumbled from one of the hamburgers they had ordered, she and her husband sued. Contending that the condiment was hazardous to the customer, the Swansons said the fast-food corporation breached an implied warranty for safety. Janella asked for $110,000, and her husband, Harold, requested $15,000 to compensate for the loss of services and companionship of his spouse.

The Swansons and the Golden Arches settled out of court. The McDonald's affiliate in Knoxville said it made no monetary payment to the plaintiffs, and it admitted no wrongdoing in the April 2001 settlement. Other details are confidential.

GROUND OR WHOLE BEAN?

Maybe burning your chin on a hot pickle isn't the worst thing that can happen to you in a restaurant. Ask Toronto's George Arlette, who is suing coffee king Starbucks Corp. for $1.5 million. Arlette, thirty-seven, claims that in August 1999 his penis was smashed by a faulty toilet seat at a Starbucks in Manhattan's Chelsea district. He filed suit in New York four months later.

How can such a thing happen? Are you sitting down? C. F. Kovacs, Arlette's attorney, told Reuters that his client "was in a seated position on the toilet when he turned to retrieve the toilet paper in back of the seat—when the seat shifted, causing his penis to be caught and crushed between the seat and the bowl."

Arlette's suit alleges the java giant carelessly allowed "a defective toilet seat to remain open . . . causing a hazardous and unsafe condition . . . in its public restrooms." As a result of this carelessness, Arlette claims, he suffered a "crushed penis, Peyronie's disease, retrograde ejaculation with consequent substantial reduction in sperm count, infertility, severe bruising to his penis, and sexual function impairment." (In severe cases, Peyronie's disease causes pain and forces the penis to bend or arc during an erection.)

Arlette is asking for $1 million in damages and his wife Susan, who has been "deprived of his services," asks for the other half-million. "It was supposed to be a romantic holiday," she said of their ill-fated trip to the Big Apple.

TRY THE MAGIC 8-BALL

Francis T. Hamilton of Roanoke, Virginia, claimed that he paid Lisa Mae Reardon about $75,000, including $29,000 from his retirement account. She provided him with detailed investment advice, but it didn't pan out, so he sued her for over $3 million.

Not a stockbroker or financial advisor, Miller, aka Madame Bella, was a palm reader. Hamilton said she sold him losing numbers to play in Virginia's lottery, and he sued her for the amount of a week's grand prize, which he felt was rightly his. He alleged that Madame Bella promised to use her psychic powers to pick the winning numbers, but failed to deliver.

Hamilton advised the press that Madame Bella assured him he would win the $3 million prize. "She told me that she was going to give me some numbers for the lottery. She was going to go to church and God would give her these numbers."

Judge Pat Doherty of Roanoke's circuit court decided that Hamilton had indeed been defrauded, but declined to award damages to him just for being gullible. The judge said, "No one on the planet is governed by magic, or soothsayers, or palm readers, or fortune tellers. People don't cast spells upon each other. Stars don't provide answers to routine problems of our daily life."

Madame Bella was ordered to return the seventy-five grand Hamilton had paid her. But the psychic had already folded up her tent, packed away her crystal ball, and was doing time in a federal prison. The judgment was considered unenforceable.

SHOCKING DECISION

In *Kim v. Chicago Transit Authority*, the Illinois Supreme Court affirmed a verdict in favor of Dae Soo Kim's estate, awarding $1.5 million plus interest. The family had sued the transit authority in 1992 for inadequate warnings, after Kim, who was legally drunk, was electrocuted by a "third rail."

Kim, forty-six, was on his way home from a party. His blood-alcohol level, later measured at .341, placed him in the "stupor" level of intoxication. Kim crossed onto transit authority property, apparently to urinate, and touched the rail. It carried 600 volts of electricity to supply power to the trains—and he was killed. A jury found that Kim was partly at fault, but held the Transit Authority liable for 50 percent of the plaintiff's damages of $3 million.

The court found that the Chicago Transit Authority, despite having placed substantial wooden barriers on its right-of-way, had insufficiently alerted pedestrians not to walk in that area. (It had also posted signs on sawhorses at each side of the tracks, warning "Danger," "Keep Out," and "Electric Current.")

WHO YA GONNA CALL?

In 1990 Saul and Janice Pavelka gave Doris Meyers a $32,500 down payment on her $650,000 Victorian mansion, which fronted the Hudson River in Nyack, New York. The buyers loved the huge old three-story home's mysterious feel—until a local architect informed them that their dream house was haunted. Janice was frightened, and the Pavelkas asked to back out of the deal. The seller refused to cancel the sale or return their escrow money, so they sued her.

Doris Meyers had long said the house was haunted, actively promoting it in a walking tour of ghostly dwellings in Nyack. In several publications she described the resident phantoms, one of whom was a "cheerful, apple-cheeked" spook, others who were "dressed in Revolutionary period clothing." Meyers was eager to discuss her vaporous housemates—until she decided to sell the house. Then she didn't say "boo."

The Pavelkas lost in trial court, as the judge relied on their *caveat emptor* (let the buyer beware) duty to discover flaws in the home before committing to a purchase. But the couple persisted with an appeal to the state supreme court's appellate division, and this time, they won a 3-2 decision.

The high court found that the seller "had deliberately fostered the belief that her home was possessed by ghosts." Meyers was at fault for not telling the Pavelkas about the spirits inhabiting their new digs. "Not being a 'local,'" Justice Rubin said of Saul Pavelka, the "plaintiff could not readily learn that the home he had contracted to purchase is haunted."

Justice Rubin ruled for the majority that "applying the strict rule of caveat emptor to a contract involving a house possessed by poltergeists conjures up visions of a psychic or medium routinely accompanying the structural engineer and Terminix man on an inspection of every home subject to a contract of sale. It portends that the prudent attorney will establish an escrow account lest the subject of the transaction come back to haunt him and his client—or pray that his malpractice insurance coverage extends to supernatural disasters. In the interest of avoiding such untenable consequences, the notion that a haunting is a condition which can and should be ascertained upon reasonable inspection of the premises is a hobgoblin which should be exorcised from the body of legal precedent and laid quietly to rest."

The Pavelkas had their deposit returned, and Doris Meyers eventually sold the house and moved to Florida. A 1995 book, Sir George, *The Ghost of Nyack* (Deer Publishing), recounts a series of conversations with the spectral occupants.

FELINE FILIBUSTER

Everett and Kathleen Bush were owners of a feline they called "Blackie the Talking Cat." Everett Bush testified in court that Blackie "was talking when he was six months old, but I could not prove it then. It was where I could understand him, but you can't understand him. It took me altogether a year and a half before I had him talking real plain where you could understand him."

Bush brought Blackie before an adoring public when the talented tabby spoke, for a fee, on radio and on television shows such as "That's Incredible." When his fame began to subside, Blackie and the Bush family moved to Augusta, Georgia, where they accepted "contributions" that some paid to hear Blackie speak. After receiving several complaints, the Augusta police insisted that Everett and Kathleen must purchase a business license.

They sued, challenging the constitutionality of Augusta's Business License Ordinance. Their complaint alleged that the ordinance (which contained no category for speaking animals) was inapplicable, vague, and overbroad, and that it violated Blackie's rights of free speech and association. The district court found in favor of the Augusta City Council and the court of appeals affirmed.

The appeals court noted that Blackie's "elocutionary endeavors were entirely intended for pecuniary enrichment" and were not an expression of free speech. It said, "Blackie would become catatonic and refuse to speak whenever his audience neglected to make a contribution." The court concluded that it would "not hear a claim that Blackie's right to free speech has been infringed. First, although Blackie arguably possesses a very unusual ability, he cannot be considered a 'person' and is therefore not protected by the Bill of Rights. Second, even if Blackie had such a right, we see no need for appellants to assert his right (on his behalf). Blackie can clearly speak for himself."

TWO CENTS WORTH

The *San Francisco Examiner* reported in 1994 that a judge across the bay in Oakland called a halt to William Earl's open access to California's courts. After Earl filed his forty-ninth "frivolous" petition since 1987, the judge said enough was enough.

It's hard to pick a favorite among Earl's many, many previous lawsuits, but here's one: A grocery store had accepted Earl's coupon that was good for thirty cents off on a purchase of Mug Root Beer, but charged him sales tax on the posted price. This had the unintended consequence of reducing his take by two pennies, to twenty-eight cents, and he sued.

MOMMIES BEWARE . . .

In December 2001 Menusaver, Inc., an affiliate of J.M. Smucker Co., sued Albie's Foods, Inc. It alleged that Albie's sold crust-less peanut butter and jelly sandwiches in violation of Menusaver's patent. That's right, somebody else was selling PB&J sandwiches *without the crusts*, and that stuck in their craw.

In 1999 Menusaver had been awarded U.S. Patent 6,004,596 for a "sealed crust-less sandwich. The sandwich includes a lower bread portion, an upper bread portion, an upper filling and a lower filling between the upper and lower bread portions . . . The upper and lower fillings are preferably comprised of peanut butter and the center filling is comprised of at least jelly. The center filling is prevented from radiating outwardly into and through the bread portions from the surrounding peanut butter." The "Uncrustables®" page of Smucker's website explains that it "has discovered a new way to seal homemade goodness into a peanut butter and jelly sandwich . . . without the crust!" *Discovered.*

Albie's began serving crust-less PB&J sandwiches in 2000. That December, Smucker's attorney sent Albie's a letter stating that the Albie's sandwich was a clear infringement of the Menusaver patent. It said Albie's must cease and desist in a jiffy. Then the lawsuits began to spread.

Parents everywhere, be warned. Don't let any lawyers find your kids with crust-less peanut butter and jelly sandwiches in their school lunchboxes.

PART FOUR

School Days, School Days, Good Old Golden Rule Days

Some students drink
at the fountain of knowledge.
Others just gargle.
–E.C. McKenzie

MAYBE HE SHOULD TRY LAW SCHOOL

Michael Harper flunked out of medical school at the University of New Mexico, and then sued the school for failing to accommodate him under the Americans with Disabilities Act (ADA). His disability, Harper claimed, is that he doesn't do well on exams because they make him nervous.

When Harper entered medical school in 1992, he had a Ph.D. in psychology and other degrees in chemistry and biology. Harper told his professors that he had an "anxiety disorder" during tests, but didn't need any special treatment. However, he did poorly in several subjects. Harper left the school and filed suit, claiming that the university should recognize his test anxiety as a protected disability.

The district court granted summary judgment for the school, stating that Harper was not disabled under the ADA. He appealed, but lost again. Educators were gratified that the Tenth Circuit Court of Appeals upheld the position that an impairment related to certain stressful situations is not a disability. Requiring the school to pass Harper on to the next level of the program would represent an unreasonable accommodation, the appellate court concluded.

His lawyers appealed to the United States Supreme Court, which ultimately said it would not hear the case. The high court rejected Harper's claim that UNM should have recognized his "test anxiety disorder" as a protected disability.

THE CHRISTIAN THING TO DO

Florida reverend Wendell Grace and his wife, Sallie Ann Grace, filed a $160,000 lawsuit against Southeastern Guide Dogs, Inc., in 1995. Each plaintiff sought $80,000 in damages; the wife for loss of earnings, physical and mental pain and suffering, shame, humiliation and embarrassment, and a subsequent inability to lead a normal life; the reverend for loss of his spouse's care and company.

The well-respected school raised and trained guide dogs for use, at no cost, by the blind and visually impaired. But Arleigh Turnwood, an indigent blind man, stepped on Sallie Ann's toe, possibly breaking it, while he was learning to use Freddy, one of the school's new graduates. Turnwood and Freddy had been practicing with an instructor in a shopping mall. Witnesses told the *Houston Chronicle* that Sallie Ann made no effort to get out of the blind man's way because "[I] wanted to see if the dog would walk around me." Sallie Ann admitted that she had stopped in front of them to see if the dog would avoid her. It pulled over to one side, but Turnwood, unaccustomed to Freddy's warnings, stepped on Sallie Ann's foot. Thirteen months later, the Graces filed suit against the guide dog group.

The public outrage overwhelmed the couple, and they withdrew their suit "with prejudice" (they may not re-file). The Graces' lawyers made a charitable contribution to Southeastern Guide Dogs.

TENNIS, ANYONE?

In 1989 a female student was the first girl to go out for the football team at Francis Scott Key High School in Union Bridge, Maryland. Upon advice of its attorneys, the school reluctantly permitted Donetta Lowell, seventeen, to try out for the team under Title IX, a federal statute that bars gender discrimination in schools that receive federal funding.

Donetta had never played organized football, but was given a uniform and went to practice as a running back. On her team's first scrimmage, she was tackled and suffered massive internal injuries, including damage to her spleen and pancreas. In October 1992 she filed a $1.2 million lawsuit against the Carroll County Board of Education, claiming that the school failed to inform her of how dangerous football is.

On April 7, 1994, a three-judge panel dismissed Donetta's suit. The Court of Special Appeals ruled that the school had no duty to warn her that she might be injured while playing football.

PLAYING HARDBALL

In 2001 Pennsylvania teenager Aileen Perkins sued her former softball coach, alleging that he stunted her athletic development and wrecked her chances of a college scholarship. Her lawyers, possibly in a search for deeper pockets, also sued the Middletown Athletic Association and four softball league directors for $700,000.

Perkins claimed that softball coach Bill Szabo knowingly taught her a controversial pitch because it won games. This, she said, caused her emotional distress and damaged her reputation. He also used "favorite players," she complained.

When Aileen was eleven, her parents had hired Szabo to teach pitching in the basement of his home. By the Perkins' account, he taught her a pitch that was later ruled illegal. If the pitch was illegal, the coach's lawyers asked, why didn't she just change coaches, or pitching styles, or both?

The defendants' attorneys told the media that, even if unsuccessful, the suit would scare away volunteer coaches. "All these volunteers who help out in leagues will say, 'Why bother? I don't need the aggravation.'"

MUST NOT HAVE BEEN A PHYSICS MAJOR

A freshman at the University of Idaho lived in a dormitory whose windows overlooked the street below. One afternoon, to get the attention of a couple of friends passing by, Neil Bowers decided to "moon" them. He climbed over his radiator and up to the window, dropped his drawers, leaned his shiny hiney against the glass—and kept going right through the window, backwards. The young scholar dropped three floors, smacked the ground, and suffered compression fractures and a broken vertebra. He also had deep cuts and bruises on his hands and lower body.

He left the university and went home to convalesce. Months later, perhaps as part of the healing process, he sued the school for not warning dorm residents of the risks inherent in windows on the upper floors. Some of the university's students at the time placed tongue-in-cheek signs on the building, warning the unsuspecting not to butt up against the windows.

To add insult to injury, a local newspaper pointed out that the flying frosh was not drunk at the time he fell. Bowers had asked for almost a million dollars in his 1994 suit, but it was dismissed.

AIR BALL

In April 1999 Louie Collister, seventeen, was ticketed for riding in a car with open alcohol containers. A month later, while driving under the influence, he smashed into a tree and nearly killed himself. This time, Collister was also hit with a DUI conviction. A star basketball player and senior at suburban Chicago's Warren Township High School, Collister was then kicked off the team for two alcohol-related violations of the school's athletic code.

The teenager tossed a suit against his school district that was as desperate as a shot from mid-court. Claiming protection as an alcoholic under Section 504 of the Rehabilitation Act and under the Americans with Disabilities Act, Collister sought reinstatement on the team and $100,000 in damages. His attorney also said the suspension jeopardized Collister's chances for an athletic scholarship.

U.S. District Judge Paul Plunkett blocked the shot. Section 504 includes a provision specifically permitting schools to sanction students who drink. In addition, the school district revoked Collister's athletic eligibility before its officials knew he had been diagnosed an alcoholic. Therefore, the revocation of eligibility was not due to the alleged disability.

WALKING ON EGGSHELLS

One of the cases many law school students learn is a famous action, *Vosburg v. Putney*. In that classic 1891 case from Wisconsin, one schoolboy kicked another in the shin, causing unexpectedly major injuries to the victim. The courts held that the kicker could be held liable because he intended to cause wrongful contact, regardless of the fact that he did not intend to cause injury. This is known as the eggshell skull rule (the wrongdoer is responsible even if his victim has some unusual and unknown vulnerability).

According to the University of Virginia's *Cavalier Daily*, P. J. Isaacs, a prominent torts scholar, was explaining Vosburg to the class in which first-year law student Gloria Cruz was enrolled. The professor indicated the case's legal principles meant he should not do what he was about to demonstrate, and he momentarily touched his student's clothed shoulder lightly.

In February 2002 Cruz filed a claim of assault and battery, asking $25,000 in compensatory damages and $10,000 in punitive damages from Professor Isaacs. She was particularly concerned that she would be required to take a second class from him.

"What some would characterize as mere touching to this victim was an extreme event," her lawyer said. "What makes it different is that she was the victim at the hands of men in the past."

I WILL NOT SMOKE IN SCHOOL.
I WILL NOT SMOKE IN SCHOOL.
I WILL NOT SMOKE IN SCHOOL.
I WILL NOT SMOKE IN SCHOOL.
I WILL NOT SMOKE IN SCHOOL.
I WILL NOT SMOKE IN SCHOOL.

Dave Carlson had taught school for thirty years and he'd seen a lot of kids misbehave. But this time he was really fuming—over a student smoking in the bathroom. A math teacher at Liverpool High School in New York, Carlson caught eleventh-grader Will O'Day smoking in the boys' bathroom. Sending Will to the principal's office wasn't enough; Carlson sued the student in 1999.

The teacher's suit asked for fifty-seven dollars for a doctor's visit and allergy medication that Carlson claimed he needed after he was exposed to the smoke. In small claims court he also asked for an unspecified amount in punitive damages for pain and suffering. Symptoms apparently included a sore throat, headache, watery eyes, and congestion.

The school board suspended the litigious lecturer, though neither side would comment on the reasons for the disciplinary action. He was then reassigned outside the classroom. Carlson eventually dropped his suit against the young nicotine fiend, but sued the school district in 2001 over his reassignment.

PART FIVE

It's Not About the Money

Litigation is the basic legal
right which guarantees every
corporation its decade in court.

–David Porter

Judgement
TOTAL
$$$$$$$

HOW MUCH IS THAT KITTY IN THE AIRPLANE?

In September 2002 the Associated Press reported that Leonard Hoffman and Connie Ford had filed a $5 million lawsuit against Air Canada, its cargo-handling company, and certain employees at San Francisco International Airport. Wrongful death? Pain and suffering in an economy-class seat? No, the couple alleged that Air Canada lost their cat, Fu, and they wanted compensation.

Hoffman and Ford were moving from Ontario, Canada, to San Francisco with fifteen-year-old Fu and four other cats. Fu and the other felines traveled in plastic crates approved by the airline, the suit claimed. When the plane got to San Francisco, Fu's crate had been broken and the tabby was gone. The bereft cat lovers retained "animal rights lawyer" Robert Dumont, who had in 1991 represented the owners of two huge dogs that fatally mauled a young woman at the door to her Pacific Heights apartment.

Air Canada, the plaintiffs alleged, was guilty of negligence, negligent infliction of emotional distress, fraud, and false advertising. The suit is the largest ever filed over a cat, beamed their proud lawyer.

"It's not about the money," Hoffman insisted.

FAILURE TO COMMUNICATE

A Pitney Bowes salesman, Yakubuku Idowu, sued his employer for racial discrimination in 1996. During the contentious trial, Idowu, an African American, testified that a fellow employee had called him "Yakubuku, ooga-booga, jungle-jungle." The French-Canadian co-worker responded that he had been misunderstood; he claimed to have really said "Bonjour, bonjour."

A Los Angeles jury found that Idowu had been the victim of racial slurs at work and that he was discriminated against in terms of sales assignments because of his color. He was awarded $97,000 in lost wages, $2.5 million for emotional distress, and $8.5 million in punitive damages, for a total of about $11.1 million.

Shortly thereafter, Los Angeles Superior Court Judge M. H. Mackey overturned the award, citing a responsibility to protect businesses from runaway jury verdicts. Mackey found the jury's award "disproportionate to the injuries" and "so unsupported by the evidence that it shocks the conscience of this court." The plaintiff said he would appeal.

BUSTED!

An attorney from Augusta, Georgia, was so perturbed by unsolicited fax advertisements his office had received from a local Hooters restaurant that he filed a class action suit in 1995.

Richard Maston told the *Augusta Chronicle* that "he brought the case against Hooters not for money but to make a point." Other small businesses that advertised the same way were not included in the suit, however, prompting speculation that the attorney knew better than to try to milk a local advertiser without the deep pockets of a chain of hundreds of breastaurants.

Six years later, a jury determined that Hooters had "willfully or knowingly" faxed a half-dozen unsolicited advertisements to each of the 1,320 class members. Damages of $11.9 million were assessed, including about $6000 for each plaintiff. The lawyers received $4 million—racking up 667 times the amount the individual clients were awarded.

"This is not a legitimate consumer protection case," a Hooters official told *Good Morning America*. "Congress never intended that a lawyer representing a single plaintiff could use this statute to recover on behalf of a thousand or more people who have never raised any complaint, to drive a local business into bankruptcy and obtain a $4 million fee."

Hooters unsuccessfully appealed the huge award, which apparently was the largest ever under the federal junk fax laws. Hooters of Augusta filed for bankruptcy.

MOVIN' ON UP

In 1995, Bridgit Howards agreed to an undisclosed out-of-court settlement from the city of Victoria, British Columbia. She had sued the Canadian city for injuries suffered when an officer accidentally shot her during a police raid.

Howards, twenty-three, had asked for approximately $200,000, of which 25 percent was for loss of earnings. Her profession? She was a prostitute at the time, an occupation that Howards said was but a springboard to her new career as an exotic dancer.

(Better than sending faxes for Hooters.)

DON'T SPEND IT ALL IN ONE PLACE

Washington's National Center for Public Policy Research reported in 1997 on a class action lawsuit that involved the wording on monthly credit card bills. The lawyers representing the class were awarded $140,000 when the credit card company decided that it would be cheaper for them to settle than to go to trial

One of the plaintiffs, Roberta Younger, disclosed to the *San Diego Business Journal* the amount that she and thousands of others were awarded: exactly ninety-three cents.

Younger was still not happy, even though she had "ninety-three cents to blow." Her bank, she said, "spent countless hours dealing with the lawsuit. The legal fees and administrative costs to issue thousands of ninety-three-cent checks were ultimately passed on to customers. In fact, just issuing this check cost more than I received. This is time and money that could have been spent making the bank more competitive and consumer-friendly." Younger surmised that the lawyers based the suit not on "a desire to seek change in the best interest of the 'wronged' class, but rather on a desire to capture a big settlement."

HOW'S YOURS, DEAR?

Daniel Barron of Massapequa, New York, sued a local lunch counter in 1991 to recover a "food sharing" fee he was charged. The charge amounted to $1.50.

Apparently, Barron tasted the soup that his wife had ordered, and she took a bite of his meatloaf sandwich. Barron said: "If the food is mine, I should be able to determine the use of it. Or are they only leasing it to us?"

He later claimed to have won the small claims case for the $1.50 sharing charge (plus tax) and court costs of $5.50.

SIC 'EM, TABBY

Pete Morales just wanted to use the library. On November 16, 2000, he walked into the public facility in Escondido, California, with his assistance dog, Kimba, a fifty-five-pound Labrador mix. Morales says they were attacked in a vicious and unprovoked manner by the library's twelve-pound mascot, L.C., aka Library Cat. Morales sued the town for $1.5 million, claiming that the feline's brutality caused him to suffer a panic attack and physical impairments.

Morales, who suffers from several disabilities including chronic pain syndrome and borderline personality disorder, acted as his own attorney. He claimed that he spent forty-six dollars in veterinary treatment for Kimba (scratched nose) and another thirty-eight dollars on chiropractic care for himself. The rest of the one and one-half million bucks was for punitive damages.

In August 2002 a superior court judge tentatively dismissed almost all of Morales' suit, including his contention that the city violated a criminal hate-crime law. The court allowed only his allegation that his right of equal access to public facilities with his assistance dog was violated.

The assistant city attorney said it was always the library's policy to permit any assistance animal in the library. "The problem was a cat with its own feline whims."

FORGIVE US OUR TRESPASSES

Michigan's Empire Mine, one of the nation's largest iron ore producers, was originally developed in the 1870s. It runs round-the-clock and is the area's largest civilian employer.

Bruce T. Warrington and over fifty other plaintiffs then living near the mine sued its owners, Cleveland-Cliffs Iron Co., in 1992 complaining of "dust, noise, and vibrations coming from the mine." They sought damages for, of all things, *trespassing* by the dust. A jury returned a verdict in favor of most of the plaintiffs on the trespass claim, awarding damages of about $600,000.

The company appealed, arguing that dust does not meet the traditional requirements for a trespass complaint.

The Michigan Court of Appeals concluded that this case sounded like a nuisance complaint, not trespassing, since "the law of trespass in Michigan does not cover airborne particulate, noise, or vibrations . . ." The award was overturned.

I'M REALLY, REALLY SORRY; NOW PAY UP

Gerald Lyons worked as a model in Winston cigarette advertising for two years in the late 1970s. The *Washington Times* reported in April 2002 that Lyons was suing R.J. Reynolds Tobacco, Winston's manufacturer, for $65 million.

Lyons said he had become stressed by the role he played in causing cancer and other smoking-related diseases in people who saw the ads he appeared in. In a federal lawsuit filed in Little Rock, Arkansas, Lyons asked $65 million from the tobacco company because he suffered from "long episodes of remorse and guilt."

Warnings had been printed on cigarette packages for roughly twenty years when Lyons was shilling for Winston.

"STRONG ENOUGH FOR A MAN, BUT MADE FOR A CHIHUAHUA"

Nature Labs sells fragrances for animals. Among its perfumes, found in pet and novelty stores, was "Tommy Holedigger," a parody of products by popular designer Tommy Hilfiger. As the *New York Law Journal* reported in 2002, Hilfiger sued.

The spoof product's name was changed to "Timmy Holedigger," and the packaging was altered to look less like Hilfiger's. But under the new logo was the phrase, "If you like Tommy Hilfiger, your pet will love Timmy Holedigger." Hilfiger said that was false advertising and claimed that Holedigger was a competing product that was trading on Hilfiger's good will.

In *Tommy Hilfiger Licensing Inc., v. Nature Labs LLC*, Hilfiger lost. Judge Michael B. Mukasey ruled that the perfume could not possibly be confused with Tommy Hilfiger cologne. "There is nothing to suggest that a designer label has anything to lose from mere association with pets, particularly where the entire association is a light-hearted if somewhat heavy-handed parody," Mukasey wrote.

The judge noted that other trademark holders have not challenged such parody scents for pets as Pucci (Gucci), Bono Sport (Ralph Lauren's Polo Sport) and Miss Claybone (Liz Claiborne). "Hilfiger fails to see the humor in all this," Mukasey wrote, cautioning that the designer's company "is advised to chill."

PART SIX

What's Up, Doc?

Doctors are the same as lawyers; the only difference is that lawyers merely rob you, whereas doctors rob you and kill you too.

—Anton Chekhov

SOME PEOPLE HAVE ALL THE LUCK

The Associated Press reported in April 1996 that Circuit Judge Patrick J. Madden threw out Rose Carlino's lawsuit against St. Florian Catholic Church, the State of Wisconsin, and a physicians' insurance company. Carlino, seventy-three, claimed she had incurred injuries that cost her $90,000 six years earlier when the Milwaukee church's 300-pound electronic bingo board fell off a stage and landed on her. Wait, there's more.

According to the plaintiff, the church's negligence caused her to suffer from unusual side effects including spontaneous orgasms, sometimes multiple orgasms. She also found herself to be sexually attracted to women for the first time.

Judge Madden tossed her suit because Carlino repeatedly refused to take the psychological exam he had ordered. (Madden's decision was affirmed on appeal in 1997.)

A lawyer for St. Florian's told the court, "It is unexplained in modern medicine how a bump on the head can alter sexual orientation or cause recurring orgasms."

THE DEVIL'S HANDIWORK

A Virginia construction worker, Rondell Emerson, was operating a circular saw when he claimed to see the sign of the devil on his hand. Possibly remembering the biblical phrase "if thy hand offend thee, cut it off . . ." (Mark 9:43), Emerson sawed his hand off at the wrist.

His horrified co-workers had him (and the hand, packed in ice) flown immediately to a nearby hospital, where Emerson gave his initial consent to have it reattached. Shortly thereafter, Emerson changed his mind and denied consent, preferring to do battle single-handed against Satan. A judge informed waiting plastic surgeon Joseph Sprague that if he reattached the hand without permission he could face charges of criminal assault and battery. It remained severed.

The patient then sued Sprague for malpractice, alleging that the doctor should have known he was not capable of either giving or denying consent. A jury found that Sprague acted correctly after Emerson withdrew consent, and the $144,000 suit was dismissed.

ALLEGATIONS OF MALPRACTICE

In 1999 controversial attorney and radio talk-show host Geoffrey Fieger was slapped by the Michigan Court of Appeals for misconduct that was "truly egregious—far exceeding permissible bounds." He had brought a $15 million malpractice suit against Troy's William Beaumont Hospital and cardiologist Dr. Michael Green. Fieger said his client, Rick Toscano, thirty-six, suffered a heart attack and was rushed to the hospital, where he lingered in bed for nine hours before being treated. The higher court overturned a jury trial verdict in Fieger's favor.

During the trial, Fieger had "repeatedly and with no basis in fact accus[ed] defendants and their witnesses of engaging in conspiracy, collusion, and perjury to cover up their alleged malpractice," the appeals court said. He "insinuated, outrageously, and with no supporting evidence that Dr. Green 'abandoned' [the patient] to engage in a sexual tryst with a nurse."

Fieger, who had been the unsuccessful Democratic candidate for governor the year before, called the court's unanimous ruling a "laughable decision by three henchmen" (of Governor Engler, his opponent). He threatened to file misconduct charges against all three jurists.

On a number of occasions Fieger has won jury verdicts, only to have them tossed out on appeal. Of these frequent reversals by appellate courts, Fieger told the *Detroit Free Press*, "It's not a wild, paranoid delusion. It's a conspiracy to get me."

SHOO FLY DON'T BOTHER ME

In 1941 the U.S. Attorney's office in Buffalo, New York, brought suit over an allegedly misbranded drug product. The suit was entitled:

UNITED STATES

v.

11 1/4 DOZEN PACKAGES OF ARTICLE LABELED IN PART MRS. MOFFAT'S SHOO FLY POWDERS FOR DRUNKENNESS.

The court explained that use of the words "for drunkenness" on the label "was the equivalent of saying that the article was a cure, mitigation, treatment, or prevention of drunkenness within statute defining a drug as an article intended for use in the diagnosis, cure, mitigation, treatment, or prevention of disease."

On behalf of the government, five physicians testified that the product's key ingredients, antimony and potassium tartrate (tartar emetic), had no positive effect on drunkenness. In fact, the doctors said, tartar emetic was dangerous when administered orally, and standard textbooks treated it as a poison. One of the manufacturer's officers testified only that people had used it for years and nobody had complained.

The court concluded that the label was false and misleading, and that the drug was dangerous when used at the dosage prescribed on the label. "Shoo Fly Powder for Drunkenness" was swatted.

THE LARGEST FRAUD SCHEME EVER

In a suit against cigarette maker Philip Morris, Inc., in late 2002, a superior court jury in Los Angeles awarded Judy Farmer $750,000 in economic damages and $100,000 for pain and suffering. Farmer, sixty-four, was diagnosed with lung cancer, which later spread to her liver. She had started smoking at seventeen.

The twelve-person jury then made a colossal punitive damages award: $28 BILLION. (For perspective, that's about the annual gross national product of oil-rich Kuwait.) Previously, the largest individual jury award against a tobacco company was $3 billion (won by a former heroin addict with cancer). That was later reduced to "only" $100 million.

The attorney for Philip Morris' told the court, "If she had stopped smoking . . . even in the 1980s, she would not have lung cancer today." Farmer's attorney countered that the tobacco giant concealed the health risks of cigarettes in "the largest fraud scheme ever perpetrated by corporations anywhere."

"It's really open season on the industry," Richard Daynard, a law professor and tobacco expert, told the Associated Press. Farmer's lawyer "only asked for $20 billion. It's funny to say, but that's all he asked for." Financial analysts expect the award to be reduced.

THE DEVIL MADE ME DO IT

In 1986 Beth Verdon, a Wisconsin nurse's aide, was treated by psychiatrist James Connover. According to *Scientific American*, she had sought his help in coping with a traumatic event her daughter had experienced. Instead, Dr. Connover apparently used psychotherapeutic techniques including hypnosis to unearth buried memories of rape and childhood abuse that Verdon herself had experienced. Verdon came to believe that she had over 120 personalities—some were children, some adults, some angels, one was Satan and a one a duck

(Because he had to help so many personalities, Connover said creatively, he invoiced her insurance company for group therapy.)

Verdon also began to remember having eaten babies, having been in a satanic cult, having fornicated with animals, and much more. Leaving no stone unturned, the good doctor performed hours-long exorcisms on Verdon, sprinkling holy water on her and screaming for Satan to vacate her being.

She eventually concluded that these memories were false—planted by Dr. Connover. Verdon sued him for malpractice, and after a five-week trial the lawsuit was settled out of court for $2.4 million.

BAD MEDICINE

From across the Atlantic, London's *Daily Telegraph* reports on a disturbing 2002 case.

Maurice Sheldon is claiming up to £100,000 (about $150,000) in compensation for lost wages after being sacked by Lancashire's Victoria Blackpool Hospital. He says the dismissal is unfair and is suing the hospital.

Sheldon, a surgeon, was struck from the medical register after having been found responsible for the deaths of four patients and the severe injuries of six others. The General Medical Council found him guilty of serious professional misconduct, repeated incompetence, and an entrenched misinterpretation of his own abilities. They concluded that Sheldon had badly mismanaged ten operations—one liver surgery, four bowel surgeries, and five breast reductions.

Sheldon is demanding compensation for his loss of salary and for damages from being fired improperly. His nickname, as reported in the British press, is "Dr. Botch."

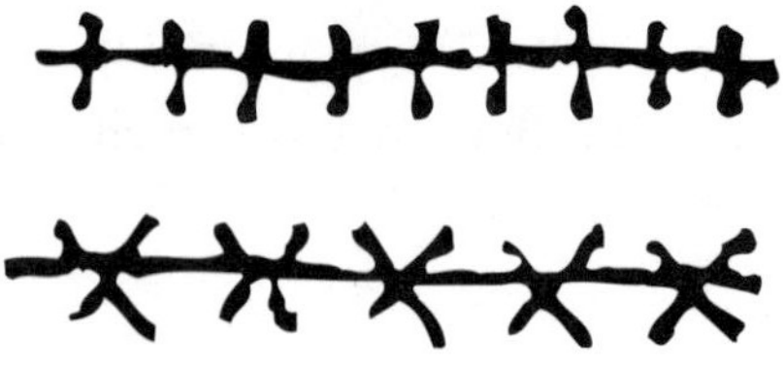

BLOOD-SUCKING INSECTS

In March 2001 federal prosecutors indicted former Democratic Congressman Ed Mezvinsky on some sixty counts of fraud and related offenses. Authorities said Mezvinsky cheated investors out of about $10.4 million. Apparently, he was trying to make up his losses after falling for a commonplace advance-payments e-mail scam.

The indictment said Mezvinsky incurred huge personal and business reverses while working as an attorney in the late '80s and '90s. To meet his expenses, Mezvinsky allegedly made false statements to financial institutions, forged bank documents, and swindled money from his clients. But it wasn't his fault.

Mezvinsky claims his misbehavior stemmed from psychiatric side effects of an anti-malaria medication, Lariam, which he took on his frequent business trips to Africa. He claims his long-term use of Lariam brought on psychiatric disorders that made him invest poorly and eventually lose the money (some of which was an inheritance belonging to his wife—a former congresswoman). Mezvinsky is suing the pharmaceutical giant Roche AG, Philadelphia's Presbyterian Medical Center, his doctor, and a pharmacy. They should reimburse the losses of the people who entrusted their money to him, Mezvinsky claims. And pay him damages. "Clearly the responsibility lies with the manufacturers," his lawyer told the *Philadelphia Daily News*.

Roche says the drug is safe and is fighting the suit.

PART SEVEN

Traffic Jam in the Courtrooms

Discourage litigation. Persuade your neighbors
to compromise whenever you can.
Point out to them how the nominal winner is often
a real loser—in fees, expenses, and waste of time.
As a peacemaker the lawyer has a superior
opportunity of being a good man.
There will still be business enough.

—Abraham Lincoln

YOUR TAX DOLLARS AT WORK

A 1988 traffic accident left Trent Quarles injured, and he sued the village of Hanover Park, Illinois. Quarles had borrowed a motorcycle from a friend and run into an unmarked road abutment. Paralyzed from the waist down, Quarles sued the Chicagoland suburb of 35,000 residents for failing to adequately warn drivers of the median strip.

Despite the fact that he did not have a proper license and had been drinking, Quarles won. A judgment against the village of $7.2 million was reduced by 10 percent because of Quarles' contributory negligence.

The Illinois Supreme Court denied an appeal by Hanover Park. According to the *Chicago Tribune*, the village board announced in 1996 that it would have to raise property taxes by 5 percent for the next fifteen years to satisfy the judgment.

YOU DESERVE A BRAKE TODAY

In another case targeting McDonald's, *New Jersey Lawyer* reported in 1993 that the fast-food colossus had been sued unsuccessfully over an automobile accident in the Garden State. Doug Carroll pulled up to a drive-through window under the Golden Arches. He secured a chocolate milkshake between his legs; set his burger, chicken nuggets, and French fries on the passenger seat; and then headed out. When he leaned over to get some fries, Carroll unintentionally squeezed his legs together, popping the lid off the shake cup and spilling half the icy contents into his lap. Stunned and distracted, Carroll rammed his vehicle into the car in front of him.

The second car was driven by Craig Williamson, who was apparently unimpressed by Carroll's shaky tale. Williamson sued Carroll and McDonald's for damages, saying the restaurant should have cautioned Carroll of the perils of eating while driving.

The lawsuit was dismissed, with the judge finding that it would be unreasonable to blame a fast-food restaurant for negligent eating and driving by its customers. But the court rejected the burger giant's request that the plaintiff reimburse McDonald's for $10,000 in lawyer's fees. The judge said Williamson was "creative and imaginative and shouldn't be penalized for that." The lower court's rulings were affirmed on both Williamson's appeal and McDonald's cross-appeal.

IN FLAGRANTE DELICTO

British actress Gillian Taylforth was a star in the British Broadcasting Corporation's hit television series *EastEnders*. In 1994 she testified that her fiancé, Geoffrey Knights, had experienced a gastrointestinal attack on a public road, the A1. Taylforth said she comforted Knights by leaning across the front seat of their car to massage his tummy with her hands. A police officer disagreed, testifying that she was performing oral sex.

The judge permitted the jury to observe a demonstration in the courthouse parking lot. The couple went to the vehicle in question, took their seats, and fastened their seatbelts. Taylforth then showed the jurors her healing techniques. She lost.

Taylforth filed a libel suit against the *Sun* newspaper for reporting the incident according to the policeman's interpretation. During the suit, the newspaper's lawyer showed a home video in which the actress demonstrated a "party trick" featuring a good-sized sausage. She lost again.

LOVE TRAIN

In more news of looking for love in all the wrong places, Steven Adams and Karen Quintana were injured at a New York City subway station when a train plowed into them as they were having sex on a mattress—on the tracks. After the 1992 accident, Adams lost a part of one foot and suffered neck damage and a dislocated pelvis. Fortunately, Quintana was not badly hurt. Injuries to the homeless couple would have been more severe, were it not for the quick, possibly life-saving reactions of subway motormen.

According to a story in the *New York Daily News*, Adams and Quintana then sued the Transit Authority for $10 million. The amorous pair, who—to repeat—were having sex on the train tracks, accused the Transit Authority of "carelessness, recklessness, and negligence." Their lawyer explained, "Homeless people are allowed to have sex, too."

(The plaintiffs did not pursue the case and it was eventually dismissed.)

CRIME PAYS

In 1984 Donald Rawson won a $3.4 million lawsuit against East St. Louis, Illinois, for a severe beating he received from another inmate in the municipal jail. He had been held there on a minor traffic offense.

Six years later the *New York Times* reported that the bankrupt town of 48,000 had to give up its city hall to Rawson, fifty-five, as compensation. Circuit Judge Robert Scrivner awarded Rawson, who had been unable to collect otherwise, the deed to one of the city's best buildings, its four-year-old municipal hall. East St. Louis, just across the Mississippi from its more prosperous Missouri neighbor, was $55 million in debt and could not even afford city garbage collection, or radios for its few police cars.

Rawson, who suffered memory lapses and physical disabilities from the beating, was also awarded a vacant 220-acre industrial park.

APOLOGIES TO JOYCE KILMER

Albert Moore sued Jennifer Houston, Stewart Easterly, and State Farm Insurance in 1982 for damage to his "beautiful oak tree." Houston had hit the tree while driving Easterly's car, which was insured by State Farm. The defendants made a cash settlement, but when the plaintiff wanted more and sued, the Michigan trial court ruled in favor of the defendants. It said that Houston and Easterly were immune from tort liability for damage to the tree, pursuant to the no-fault insurance act.

Moore appealed to the Court of Appeals.

On behalf of a three-judge panel, Judge John H. Gillis rejected the appeal and penned the following opinion in 1983:

We thought that we would never see
A suit to compensate a tree.
A suit whose claim in tort is prest
Upon a mangled tree's behest;
A tree whose battered trunk was prest
Against a Chevy's crumpled crest;
A tree that faces each new day
With bark and limb in disarray;
A tree that may forever bear
A lasting need for tender care.
Flora lovers though we three,
We must uphold the court's decree.
Affirmed.

ANY RELATION TO THE BINGO LADY?

In a drama that Tennessee Williams might have called *A Cable Car Named Desire*, a Michigan tourist sued the city of San Francisco over an accident that had mind-boggling consequences. In 1964 Rachelle Hagan was riding on the running board of a Hyde Street cable car that hit an automobile. She was tossed around in the cable car, thrown onto the pavement, and suffered numerous cuts, bumps, and bruises. The real damage, however, went much deeper: the twenty-three-year-old dancer

said she became a nymphomaniac as a result of the accident. She sued the city, of course.

A sensational 1970s trial resulted. The plaintiff claimed that she became sexually ravenous after the accident, engaging in lovemaking as many as fifty times in five days. Hagan asked $500,000 for her physical and emotional injuries. The jury was sympathetic, but awarded her a smaller judgment.

Incidentally, now there actually is a cable car named "Desire" in San Francisco. In 1997 the Muni purchased an early-1920s streetcar from New Orleans, for use on the F-line connecting Fisherman's Wharf with Upper Market.

THE BETTER PART OF VALOR

A classic lawsuit from 1941 showcases both a fine point of the law and a judge's prose skills. The facts of *Cordas et al. v. Peerless Transp. Co. et al.* were as follows: two men had just robbed a third man at gunpoint, then the victim gave chase. One of the robbers jumped into a cab, still brandishing the pistol. He threatened the cab driver with his life, and the cabbie drove ahead. The victim ran along outside the cab and continued his pursuit. After a few moments, the terrified cab driver slammed on the brakes, and dove out of the taxi. The cab continued to move and struck a mother and her two children on the sidewalk, injuring them slightly.

Mary Cordas, the woman who was struck by the suddenly driverless taxi, sued the taxi company. Her attorneys cited the driver's failure to exercise the care and caution that a reasonable and prudent person would generally exercise under the circumstances.

The City Court of New York disagreed. It found that the driver acted under the belief that he was in mortal peril. He was not negligent when he abandoned the taxi to save his own life. The cabbie was an ordinary man, not required to exercise infallible judgment when confronted with an emergency requiring immediate action.

Justice Carlin wrote an elaborate opinion, which explained in part:

There are those who stem the turbulent current for bubble fame, or who bridge the yawning chasm with a leap for the leap's sake or who 'outstare the sternest eyes that look, outbrave the heart most daring on the earth, pluck the young sucking cubs from the she-bear, yea, mock the lion when he roars for prey' to win a fair lady, and these are the admiration of the generality of men; but they are made of sterner stuff than the ordinary man upon whom the law places no duty of emulation.

The complaint was dismissed.

PART EIGHT

Fame and Fortune

The way I see it, if you
want the rainbow, you gotta
put up with the rain.

–Dolly Parton

RUSH TO JUDGMENT

Progressive radio host Aaron Harber was sued for $20 million by conservative icon Rush Limbaugh, after Harber unveiled a talk show called "After the Rush." Limbaugh's attorney claimed that the use of the word "rush" in the title was a violation of trademark. Harber's American Civil Liberties Union attorney denied that Limbaugh owned the rights to the common word that is found in every English dictionary.

Explaining his strategy to follow Limbaugh on the air, Harber said, "We're going to listen to him and respond directly the same day. As much as my stomach will permit." The formerly rotund Limbaugh couldn't stomach the concept, and sued.

In 1996 Denver Chief Federal Judge Richard Matsch dismissed the suit. (At the time Matsch was also presiding over the trial of Oklahoma City bomber Timothy McVeigh. Matsch restored the judiciary's public image after Judge Lance Ito was perceived as bumbling through O. J. Simpson's controversial trial on murder charges.)

After gaining a measure of fame for winning the Limbaugh case, Harber changed the show's name to "Against the Rush" (at Matsch's suggestion) but Limbaugh didn't take the bait. Apparently loath to give Harber any more publicity, Limbaugh declined to rename his own show "No Safe Harber," or anything similar.

Incidentally, after the case was dismissed, Harber got his own local television show while Limbaugh's national TV show was cancelled. Limbaugh got the last laugh, however, when he signed a $250 million deal to extend his radio show while Harber stayed on public television for chicken feed.

HOW TO WIN FRIENDS AND INFLUENCE VOTERS

In May 2001, the superior court in Santa Monica, California, ordered Christopher Beach to stay at least 250 yards away from actress Nicole Kidman for three years. The court determined that he had "seriously" annoyed and harassed the star of *Moulin Rouge*, writing her a love poem and calling uninvited many times at her home, once to take her to the ballet. Beach told reporters, "She flirted with me like crazy. She gave me a knockout smile and sparkled her eyes at me. I'm a single man looking for a good woman, so I was interested."

A year later, Beach, thirty, filed a $200 million defamation suit in Los Angeles against Kidman and numerous other people and media institutions. A self-described actor-screenwriter-composer-director-producer-songwriter-entrepreneur, Beach complained that Kidman and the other defendants referred to him as a "stalker." (In a separate case, Beach is suing two airlines, claiming he was drugged and robbed on a trip to visit supermodel Claudia Schiffer. Her family called the police when he arrived at their Spanish villa.)

Beach's suit against Kidman alleges that the label "stalker" will hurt his 2004 presidential campaign.

WEE, WEE, WEE, ALL THE WAY HOME

The *Los Angeles Times* reported in 1995 that Glenn Poston had attended a Billy Joel-Elton John concert at San Diego's Jack Murphy Stadium, where a unisex bathroom policy was utilized. Poston, an attorney, then tried unsuccessfully to sue the city and the stadium for $5.4 million.

The spectacle of a woman using a urinal at the concert left him "angered, upset, embarrassed, distraught, and violated." It caused him emotional distress and embarrassment to the point that he was unable "to go." Poston said that he eventually visited a half-dozen other restrooms in the stadium, but he found women in every one. The plaintiff, too mortified to share the restrooms with the ladies, complained that he was forced to "hold it in for four hours."

The suit was dismissed, and Poston was required to reimburse the city for wasting public resources.

FROM THE BAND THAT BROUGHT YOU "PRIMAL SCREAM" AND "THEATRE OF PAIN"

In 1990 Alexander Ross attended what everybody thought was certain to be a boisterous, deafening Mötley Crüe concert in New Jersey. The veteran heavy-metal fan sat in the thirteenth row, with speakers only fifteen to twenty feet above him.

Ross said he felt a "searing pain" in his ear during a solo by lead guitarist Mick Mars. That was only halfway through the show, but Ross stayed for the entire performance. Then he sued Mötley Crüe and the concert's promoters and sponsors for $7 million because the band ruined his hearing.

In 1997 New York judge Elliot Wilk threw out the suit, saying any Mötley Crüe concertgoer knows the concert's going to be very loud. Ross assumed the risks, the judge found, and could not claim the band was negligent.

HE SUES, HE SCORES!

Some suits are too loony to pursue. At the 1994 Winter Olympics in Lillehammer, Norway, the hockey finals featured Sweden vs. Canada. With the gold medal on the line, the game was tied after overtime, so the rivals began a shootout. The game was still tied after five rounds, when Swedish star Peter Forsberg (now with the Colorado Avalanche) took the puck. He skated toward Corey Hirsch, the Canadian goalie, faked, shot, and scored a remarkable goal that proved to be the winner.

Exulting in its victory, Sweden later announced plans to commemorate the goal with a postage stamp. Hirsch, the Canadian goalie, threatened to sue the government of Sweden, protesting that the image of him outstretched in the crease, allowing Forsberg the winning goal, was "not the way I want to be remembered."

The 3.70 kronor stamp was issued in 1995 and Hirsch decided not to file suit.

WHAT'S UP WITH THAT BEAUTY AND THE BEAST?

In September 1995 a conservative Christian group based in Virginia, described certain "subliminal sex messages" that it said the Walt Disney Company had been surreptitiously placing in children's movies. The American Life League encouraged its faithful supporters to boycott the studio's products. Through e-mail and the media, the following related rumors about Disney films soon spread widely:

- *The Little Mermaid* was said to contain a scene in which a priest has an erection during a wedding ceremony (more noticeable when viewed in slow motion or frame-by-frame);
- *Aladdin* allegedly included the whispered instructions "Take off your clothes"; and
- *The Lion King* supposedly had an image in which innocent clouds and plants form the letters "S-E-X".

Charlene Hammack was outraged, so she sued Disney and Buena Vista Home Video in Arkansas State Court in 1996. On behalf of herself and "all the other residents of Washington County, Arkansas" who had acquired the offending Disney films, she alleged that the videos (and their covers) included sexual materials unsuitable for children and families. Hammack charged the defendants with invasion of privacy, fraud, negligence, and breach of warranty, and she asked for $1,000 in compensatory damages and $50,000 in punitive damages.

None of the accusations held up to close scrutiny (the "erection" appears to be a knee sticking out from a tunic), and Hammack dropped her lawsuit.

BAD AS I WANNA BE

Former National Basketball Association star Dennis Rodman is famous for his rebounding, loud parties, cross-dressing, bottle-blond hair, drunk driving, and for his stormy nine-day marriage to actress Carmen Electra. Rodman, aka The Worm, earned just a smidge more notoriety when Kent Olander, a Las Vegas casino dealer, sued him over a 1997 incident at a craps game at the Mirage.

In his suit, Olander claimed that Rodman rubbed dice on Olander's chest, stomach, bald head, and genitals before rolling them (the dice). The veteran dealer said he was humiliated and ridiculed by Rodman's "crappy" conduct. However, two other dealers testified that Rodman also rubbed them with the dice for good luck, but they were unhurt and unoffended.

Olander had initially sought $300,000 in damages, and he attempted to convince his coworkers to join the suit. "I didn't get hurt and I don't want to make money like that," one dealer said. "We're taught as children to keep our hands to ourselves," Olander's attorney argued.

In 2001 a jury in Las Vegas agreed that Olander had been rubbed the wrong way, and it ordered Rodman to pay $80,000 to the dealer.

THE AMERICAN PASTIME

In 2001 the Atlanta Braves announced that All-Star center fielder Andruw Jones was being sued. A fan said her face was injured when Jones tossed a baseball underhanded into the stands. "It's just a flip," he said of the traditional toss that gives lucky fans a coveted souvenir after the third out.

"When you come to the ballpark, you're taking a risk," Jones told the *Savannah Morning News*. "Balls and bats go into the stands all the time. What's going to happen next? If you get hit by a home run, are you going to sue the batter and the pitcher that threw the ball?"

Braves tickets include a warning to fans that balls may come into the stands.

ANOTHER FLYING FREEBIE

Robert L. Touro of Cincinnati, Ohio, was in the studio audience to see NBC's *The Tonight Show*, starring comedian Jay Leno, on September 11, 1998. During the performance of the traditional warm-up act, *Tonight Show* T-shirts were shot towards the eager audience with an air gun. Shortly thereafter, Touro, fifty-six, announced he was suing the network, the show, and Leno, claiming that he was "battered" and "forcefully struck" in the eye by an airborne shirt.

"It's not frivolous when you get hit with a hard object traveling 800 feet per second," Touro said. Representing himself, he asked for damages greater than $25,000 for his "pain and suffering, disability, lost wages, emotional distress, humiliation, and embarrassment." Touro also demanded punitive damages.

Let's do the math. Multiplying 800 feet/second times 60 seconds/minute times 60 minutes/hour; all divided by 5,280 feet/mile, equals 545 miles per hour, about the speed of a commercial jet. Sound likely to you? The T-shirt terror suit was dismissed.

I Sued Jay Leno
(and all I got was this stupid T-shirt)

ROCKIN' DOWN THE HIGHWAY

John Hartman was a founding member of the rock band the Doobie Brothers, which had such 1970s hits as "Listen to the Music," "China Grove," "Long Train Runnin'" and "Black Water." In 1994 U.S. District Judge Lowell Jensen threw out an employment discrimination suit that Hartman had filed. He wasn't suing the band, however. Hartman had asked punitive damages as a result of being denied full-time employment with the police force of Petaluma, California,

The *San Francisco Chronicle* reported that Hartman had claimed that his drug use in the early '70s made him "disabled" under the Americans with Disabilities Act (ADA). Judge Jensen ruled that Hartman had not proved that he had done enough drugs to be disabled.

Hartman said he had not taken drugs in almost twenty years. He became a reserve officer with Petaluma's police department, then applied to become a full-time cop in 1991. His application admitted to minimal previous past use of marijuana and cocaine, but the drummer was turned away from the force when an investigation disclosed a more serious drug habit. Hartman said rehabilitation from previous use of drugs is a disability under the ADA. He argued that the act protects former drug users from employment-related discrimination.

The police department contended that Hartman's application was denied in large part because he fibbed about his past drug habit. Judge Jensen ruled that the drummer's application was properly refused because he held back relevant information.

Hartman said he was unable to provide evidence of extensive drug use because all the drugs he took affected his memory.

PART NINE

A Fool for a Client

"The lawyer who represents himself has a fool for a client and a jackass for an attorney."

–Traditional

CHIVALRY IS DEAD AND THE LAWYERS HAVE KILLED IT

In August 1992 Frank Candelaria, a lawyer in southern California, sued Texaco Inc., and a local gasoline service station manager for $2 million. He alleged that the pump jockeys were discriminating against him. The station's employees, it seems, were pumping gas for women at self-service prices, but not for men.

This helpful suit was dismissed when the gas station quickly ceased the offending practice. Female customers were liberated by being forced to pump for themselves or pay full-service prices.

THE BOTTOM LINE

U.S. District Judge Robert N. Chatigny of Connecticut refused to permit lawyers to become the butt of another joke. In a 2002 ruling, he said spanking a client is not covered under legal malpractice insurance policies even if it is performed in an effort to prepare the client to testify more effectively.

Lauren Rocker claimed that her attorney, Oren Culpepper was preparing her to testify when she became nervous, rubbing her hands together repeatedly. Rocker alleged that he told her he needed to spank her so the judge wouldn't confuse her agitated behavior with deceit. After the spanking she said she would stop fidgeting and Culpepper said, "Well, I guess it worked," the admonished client claimed.

Culpepper denied the assault, but admitted that he had threatened to spank Rocker and more than a dozen other clients to render them "more afraid of him than they would be of the prosecutor." Rocker and Culpepper agreed to a $250,000 stipulated judgment in 1999, but because he was insolvent, she attempted to collect from American Home, Culpepper's insurance company. Under Judge Chatigny's ruling, the insurer was deemed not liable.

Although "the profession of the practice of law is hardly revered," American Home, admitted, "sexual assault cannot be brought under the canopy of professional services. The perverted act of intentionally fondling the bare bottoms of female clients cannot and is not part of the practice of law."

MORE NEWS FROM THE GREAT WHITE NORTH

The *Toronto Globe and Mail* reported in late 1994 that a former attorney for the Canadian House of Commons had successfully settled his lawsuit against his previous employer. Dale Harding sued the government because his job was boring.

Harding alleged that he was enticed to take a salary decrease from his previous position. He claimed that the House of Commons assured him of "exciting, challenging, and demanding" work, but, in fact, he endured "years of utter boredom."

Placed in an office with twice as many attorneys as needed, Harding had spent approximately two years twiddling his thumbs before filing his suit.

I KNOW MY RIGHTS

Peter French felt that on numerous occasions a powerful individual and his associates had caused him misery and unwarranted threats, placed deliberate obstacles in his path, and were generally responsible for his undeserved downfall. He said that these acts had deprived him of his constitutional rights, so in 1971 he filed a suit in the western district of Pennsylvania.

The defendants were SATAN AND HIS STAFF.

In his filing, French also asked the court for permission to file a complaint for violation of his civil rights *in forma pauperis* (without payment of court fees), since he claimed to be a pauper. French appeared on his own behalf, without a lawyer.

The court turned him down. District Judge Weber said even if French's "complaint reveals a prima facie recital of the infringement of the civil rights of a citizen of the United States, the Court has serious doubts that the complaint reveals a cause of action upon which relief can be granted by the court. We question whether plaintiff may obtain personal jurisdiction over the defendant in this judicial district."

The judge also observed that French failed to include with his complaint the required form with directions for the U. S. marshal to serve notice to the defendants.

MOMMY ALWAYS LOVED YOU MORE

Anthony Reno decided to represent himself in court, and why not? He was every bit as capable as opposing counsel—actually, he was opposing counsel. In fact, he was the plaintiff and the defendant, as well.

Plaintiff Anthony Reno sued himself in California's Shasta County Superior Court. Possibly to obtain favorable treatment from the IRS, Reno claimed that defendant Anthony Reno had taken control of the assets of his trust fund.

The trial court dismissed the complaint and plaintiff Reno appealed. In the California Court of Appeals' Third Appellate District, Justice Sims explained in 1985 that the result could not be unfair to Mr. Reno. "Although it is true that, as plaintiff and appellant, he loses, it is equally true that, as defendant and respondent, he wins! It is hard to imagine a more evenhanded application of justice. Truly, it would appear that [Anthony Reno] is that rare litigant who is assured of both victory and defeat regardless of which side triumphs."

Justice Sims said plaintiff Reno alleged that for over sixty years (since plaintiff/defendant was born) defendant Reno controlled the estate. Plaintiff Reno had notified defendant Reno of the trust's termination by trying to revoke his birth certificate). Sims concluded that plaintiff Reno's "birth certificate did not create a charitable trust; consequently, there was no trust which could be terminated by notice . . . here is a slam-dunk frivolous complaint."

The appeals court also considered whether respondent/defendant/beneficiary should be awarded his costs, which he could then recover from himself. Ultimately, the court affirmed the initial judgment and ordered each party to bear his own costs.

WHO ARE YOU CALLING GROTESQUE?

A Pennsylvania lawyer sued his local telephone directory in 2001 because he didn't like the looks of the ad he placed. Frank L. Cochran filed suit against the publishers of the *Westmoreland County Yellow Book* for unspecified compensatory damages and $500,000 in punitive damages.

Cochran alleged that the 2000-01 directory failed to state that he was a personal injury attorney. He also claimed that his photo in the previous edition was "so grotesque that [he] looked like an albino and discouraged any client from contacting" him.

"My fellow lawyers tease me about it," said Cochran. "What potential client would call me looking like that?"

WHAT ABOUT THOSE OTHER EIGHT LIVES?

One day in 2000 Teri Lloyd brought the family cat, Venus Viola, with her to work at the Northampton State Hospital in Massachusetts. Sadly, the curious feline was electrocuted when it came into contact with an uninsulated wire near a security trailer on the grounds.

Her husband, Ronald Lloyd, represented himself and sued Massachusetts Electric Company for the death of their pet. "Venus Viola was an extremely beautiful and brilliant black female cat who would not scratch anyone, no matter what," Lloyd wrote in his lawsuit.

Lloyd figured the cat's death was worth exactly $250,195. That works out to $195 for veterinary bills, and $250,000 because, he said, Venus Viola was a "good luck charm" who "would have gained me $250,000 had she lived."

Massachusetts Electric denied liability for the cat's death. It also denied that Venus Viola was worth a quarter-of-a-million dollars. In 2001 Hampshire Superior Court Judge Bertha Josephson urged Lloyd to settle, but he said would insist on taking the case to trial. The judge sent the case to a district court, which handles small claims and cases involving less than $25,000 in damages.

PART TEN

But It Wasn't My Fault

The fault, dear Brutus, is not in our stars,

But in ourselves . . .

–William Shakespeare,

Julius Caesar, Act 1, Scene 2.

PLAYING WITH MATCHES

In Alpena, Michigan, on August 17, 1993, a fire attributed to arson destroyed the Salem Men's Shop, owned by Nicholas Salem. Investigators found that "the fire had a single point of origin and was fueled by paper and cardboard boxes." Salem and his son initially admitted to starting the blaze, stating their intention to cause smoke damage to the store's inventory, which may not have been moving well. Although they claimed not to have planned to damage other buildings, the fire spread to the Owl Café and Ritzler's Cleaners, nearby. They later denied starting the fire, but a jury convicted the Salems of arson involving their store's building.

Salem realized he had a commercial general liability insurance policy with Frankenmuth Mutual Insurance, which sparked a thought. The convicted arsonists sued the insurance company, claiming that the fire next door was accidental, *so the company should pay* for the damages to the other building.

The trial court found for Frankenmuth, stating that there was no "occurrence" within the meaning of the policies because the Salems intentionally set the fire. The "intentional acts exclusion" barred coverage. Surprisingly, the Michigan Court of Appeals reversed the trial court's decision.

Finally, the Michigan Supreme Court unanimously reversed the court of appeal's decision. It held that torching the neighbors' buildings "was not 'accidental' as defined in the insurance policies."

THIS BUD'S FOR YOU

Marlon Dempsey sued his former employer, Anheuser-Busch, in 1996. He claimed that the Tampa brewery gave him the monthly employee perk of four free cases of beer, then canned him for alcoholism. Dempsey said that he began to have a "problem with alcohol" during the nearly four years he worked at the brewery, and that the brewer knew about his "addiction."

Anheuser-Busch said it fired him for trash-talking their brew in public. Dempsey, the company said, walked over to three patrons in a bar and advised them that he had "peed in the beer" at work. Dempsey couldn't deny his alleged remarks because he was drunk at the time. Anheuser-Busch said his comments jeopardized the beer-drinking public's faith in its products and the livelihood of its employees. So they fired him.

Dempsey, a known alcoholic, claimed that his firing violated the Americans with Disabilities Act (ADA). He also said that the brewer negligently provided him with free suds. In 1997 a federal district court in Florida rejected both claims.

The court found that the ADA provides that employers may hold alcoholics to similar standards as other employees, even when unacceptable behavior is alcohol-related. The court also held that no Florida statute established that the company had a duty to Dempsey with respect to the free beer.

WHOSE FAULT?

In a 1994 California lawsuit, the plaintiff was an attorney representing himself in the pursuit of alleged financial damages. His case was dismissed because he failed to appear for a scheduled court hearing. The attorney/plaintiff later filed another motion requesting relief from that dismissal based upon the premise that it would be unfair to penalize the client for the blunder of his lawyer.

In their opposition to this daring, if schizophrenic, motion, the defendants argued that the plaintiff "is alleging that he has caused his client [himself] irreparable harm for which he should not be made to bear the mistakes of his attorney [also himself]. Defendants, jokingly, have dubbed this the 'Sybil' defense."

The Los Angeles County Municipal Court dismissed the loony claim to shift the blame from the client to the attorney.

I THOUGHT YOU GOT IT FROM TYPING

Reuters broke a story in 1999 about a forty-year-old woman in Fort Lauderdale, Florida, who became crippled in both hands as a result of work-related activities. Carpal tunnel syndrome, also known as repetitive motion injury, was fingered as the culprit. This condition often occurs in secretaries and data-entry clerks, but the unnamed victim was a phone-sex operator who masturbated on the job to arouse her attentive clientele.

While she talked dirty to the customer, this overachiever held the phone with one hand and brought herself to climax with the other. Up to seven times a day, eager callers shared her rapture from the comfort of their own living rooms, offices, or whatever.

Our happy scene closed when the pain in her hands left the service-provider unable to reach orgasm and perform her duties. A neurosurgeon operated on her hands, resulting in $30,000 worth of medical bills, but she was still unable to get relief.

Through her attorney, she filed for workers' compensation benefits with Florida's Department of Labor and Employment Security. Claiming weekly benefits of $267 a week and reimbursement for her doctor's bills, she settled for an undisclosed amount.

WOULDN'T "SWEET FLAMING PASTRIES" BE A GOOD NAME FOR A ROCK BAND?

Rosalie Erwin of Washington Township, New Jersey, dropped a cherry Kellogg's Pop-Tart into her toaster in July 2000, then left home to drive her kids to preschool. When she got back ten or twenty minutes later, firefighters were there and smoke was billowing from the house. "Unattended food" was named by the fire department as the cause of the $100,000 blaze.

A warning on the Pop-Tarts box cautioned Erwin (and all other consumers) not to "leave the toaster appliance unattended due to possible risk of fire." But a year later, Erwin said the fire wasn't her fault, and she and her husband sued Kellogg's and Black & Decker, the toaster's manufacturer, for the hundred grand. "I never thought a Pop-Tart could turn into a blowtorch," Vincent T. Stanfill, their lawyer, told the *Philadelphia Inquirer.*

"Pop-Tarts are safe and do not cause fires," said Richard Lovell, a spokesperson for Kellogg's. "Pop-Tarts have been marketed since 1964; they have been thoroughly tested and are safe to toast and eat." On the other hand, Washington Township Fire Chief John Hoffman said he wasn't shocked that a Pop-Tart caused a fire. "Go get a Pop-Tart and try it yourself," advised the chief. "Just do it safely."

(Humorist Dave Barry wrote a column in 1993 about Pop-Tarts. He said he put the sugary snacks in a toaster and held the handle down for about six minutes until they ignited.)

In fact, the Erwin's case wasn't the first suit involving Pop-Tarts pyrotechnics. Without admitting guilt, Kellogg's paid $2,400 to the insurance company of Brad Title, an Ohio man who claimed a Pop-Tarts fire damaged his kitchen in 1992.

WHAT PART OF "DO NOT USE INDOORS" DON'T YOU UNDERSTAND?

Akron's *Beacon Journal* reported in 2002 that two carpet installers were awarded $8 million in Summit County's highest jury award ever in a product liability lawsuit. Allan Fenner and Dwayne Hill claimed they were forever scarred physically and emotionally during a fiery explosion four years earlier. And they wanted somebody else to pay.

That somebody else was Para-Chem, a South Carolina-based manufacturer of a carpet adhesive they used. Roach admitted that he had read Para-Chem's warnings that the M280 adhesive was designed exclusively for outdoor use. The men were installing carpet in a basement (indoors) when a hot water tank came on, sparking an explosion and fire that changed their lives and looks permanently.

Para-Chem attorneys argued that Fenner and Hill were to blame, not the adhesive or its labels. They said the carpet guys ignored warning labels that would have prevented the explosion. The container of adhesive was marked on the front with "All Weather Outdoor Adhesive." A side label read, "Do not use indoors because of flammability."

One of the jurors, George Duhon, said, "They didn't cover all the bases. It should jump out at you, especially if it's that dangerous. It says it's flammable, but it didn't say anything about the explosiveness and it didn't explain why you can't use it indoors." Most of the other jurors agreed, voting 6-2 to give Fenner $5 million and Hill $3 million. (They had asked for $20 million and $15 million, respectively.)

Lawyers for Para-Chem said they would appeal. "I guess it's too much to expect that people will read a label," sighed attorney Kenneth Abarrno.

ACT OF GOD

Cathy and George Pendleton just wanted to spend some time at the beach with their two kids. It didn't work out that way.

In 1994 Cathy, forty-seven, was seriously injured when she was struck by lightning on New Smyrna Beach in Volusia County, Florida. The family arrived about noon and Cathy said that as the afternoon passed, she could see a storm moving in from the south. She didn't worried about it at first, but they decided to pack up when the rain began and a "dark storm" approached. Fifteen to twenty minutes later, as they were still getting ready to leave, she was struck by a bolt from the blue.

The Pendletons filed suit against Volusia County in 1996, alleging that the county's beach lifeguards were negligent in failing to warn her of the risk of lightning. The complaint argued that the lifeguards negligently failed to call a "red light" alert until it was too late, and that they failed to warn Cathy of the danger of remaining on the beach once "red light" conditions existed.

Volusia County argued that its employees exercised reasonable care in executing the procedure, but the procedure failed to protect Cathy from a lightning strike over which they had no control. The court agreed and ruled that there was no evidence the county breached any duty to Cathy. The lifeguards' acts or omissions were not the cause of her injuries.

The Pendletons appealed, but in 2002 Florida's Fifth District Court of Appeals agreed with the lower court and affirmed.

SPF 30

PART ELEVEN

Too Loony

The difference between truth and fiction: fiction has to make sense.

–Mark Twain

DOZENS OF LOONY LAWSUITS have become legendary, and the sordid details of these disputes have spread around the world, mostly via the Internet. Problem is, they never happened, though the tales have been repeated over and over, often verbatim, as if true. These urban myths are filled with fables of idiotic plaintiffs and outrageous judgments, but the stories are fiction. Following are a few of the most widely disseminated but bogus lawsuits, essentially as they appeared on many websites:

- A jury awarded $780,000 to Bobbie Jenkins of Austin, Texas, after she broke her ankle tripping over a toddler who was running in a furniture store. The owners of the store were dismayed at the verdict, especially considering the little brat was Jenkins' own son.
- Mark Dewey of Los Angeles won $74,000 and medical expenses when his neighbor ran over his hand with a Honda

Accord. Dewey, nineteen, was trying to steal his neighbor's hubcaps and apparently didn't notice there was someone at the wheel of the car at the time.

- Clyde Bonner was leaving a Pennsylvania house he had just burglarized. He couldn't get the garage door to rise since the automatic door opener was malfunctioning. Bonner couldn't re-enter the house, either, because the door connecting the house and garage locked when he pulled it shut. The homeowners were on vacation, and Bonner found himself locked in the garage for eight days. He subsisted on a case of Pepsi and a large bag of dry dog food. Bonner sued the homeowner's insurance company, claiming the episode caused him undue mental anguish. A jury awarded him $500,000.
- A jury gave $14,500 and medical expenses to Douglas Simmons of Little Rock, Arkansas, after he was bitten on the buttocks by his next-door neighbor's beagle. The pooch was on a chain in its owner's fenced-in yard. The award was reduced from the amount Simmons had sought because the jury felt the dog might have been provoked at the time, since Simmons had shot it repeatedly with a pellet gun.
- A Philadelphia restaurant was ordered to pay $113,500 to Julia Manchester after she slipped on a soft drink and broke her coccyx. The beverage was on the floor because Manchester had thrown it at her boyfriend thirty seconds earlier during an argument.
- Mimi Fancher successfully sued the owner of a Delaware nightclub when she fell from a bathroom window to the floor

and knocked out her two front teeth. This occurred while Fancher was trying to sneak through the window in the ladies room to avoid paying the $3.50 cover charge. She was awarded $12,000 and dental expenses.

- Stanley Daggs purchased a new thirty-two-foot Winnebago motor home from a Texas dealer. On his first trip home, having entered the freeway, he set the cruise control at seventy miles per hour and calmly left the driver's seat to go into the back and made himself a cup of coffee. Not surprisingly the land yacht left the freeway, crashed, and overturned. Daggs sued Winnebago for not advising him in the handbook that he couldn't actually do this. He was awarded $1,750,000 plus a new recreational vehicle. The company changed its owner's manual as a result.

Again, not one of these last seven suits is real, and the Web is full of others just like them. *Caveat lector!*

SOURCES AND ADDITIONAL READING

PERIODICALS, NEWSPAPERS, AND OTHER NEWS MEDIA

Akron Beacon Journal

American Bar Association Journal

Arizona Daily Star

Associated Press

Augusta (Georgia) *Chronicle*

Cavalier Daily (Charlottesville, Virginia)

Chicago Tribune

Daily Telegraph (London)

Detroit Free Press

Good Morning America (ABC)

Holland (Michigan) *Sentinel*

Houston Chronicle

Los Angeles Times

New Jersey Lawyer

New York Daily News

New York Law Journal

New York Times

Philadelphia Daily News

Philadelphia Inquirer

Reuters

Rockford (Illinois) *Register-Star*

San Diego Business Journal

San Diego Union-Tribune

San Francisco Chronicle

San Francisco Examiner

Savannah Morning News

Scientific American

Scranton Times Tribune

Toronto Globe and Mail

Tucson Weekly

Washington Times

BOOKS

Adler, Bill, *First, Kill All the Lawyers: Legal Proverbs, Epitaphs, Jokes and Anecdotes*, New York, Citadel Press, 1992.

Benko, Laura B. and Attila Benko, *Buy This Book . . . Or We'll Sue You!: Outrageous Lawsuits, Outlandish Verdicts*, New York, Citadel Press, 2001.

Crier, Catherine, *The Case Against Lawyers: How Lawyers, Politicians, and Bureaucrats Have Turned the Law into an Instrument of Tyranny–and What We as Citizens Have to Do About It*, New York, Broadway Books, 2002.

Davidson, Lance S., *Ludicrous Laws & Mindless Misdemeanors: The Silliest Lawsuits and Unruliest Rulings of All Times*, New York, John Wiley & Sons, 1998.

Freedman, Warren, *Frivolous Lawsuits and Frivolous Defenses*, New York, Quorum Books, 1987.

Gregory, Leland H. III, *Presumed Ignorant!: Over 400 Cases of Legal Looniness, Daffy Defendants, and Bloopers from the Bench*, New York, Dell Publishing, 1998.

Howard, Phillip K., *The Death of Common Sense: How Law is Suffocating America*, New York, Random House, 1994.

Johnson, Kara L. and Steven R. Thompson, eds., *Blackie the Talking Cat and Other Favorite Judicial Opinions*, St. Paul, MN, West Publishing, 1996.

Liebman, Ron, *Shark Tales: True (and Amazing) Stories from America's Lawyers*, New York, Simon & Schuster, 2000.

Oliver, Quincy, *DisOrder in the Court: Funny, Frivolous, and Outrageous Lawsuits*, Minnetonka, MN, Quincy Oliver Publishing Group, 2002.

WEBSITES

http://www.atra.org/

http://www.calahouston.org/

http://www.cfif.org/htdocs/legal_issues/legal_updates/jesters_courtroom/tales.html

http://www.mlaw.org/

http://www.newsoftheweird.com/

http://overlawyered.com/

http://www.power-of-attorneys.com/

http://www.re-quest.net/g2g/humor/cases/

http://www.tildenm.com/links/greatcases.htm

http://www.truthorfiction.com/rumors/onlyinamerica.htm